# What *Really* Happened During the Middle Ages

## A Collection of Historical Biographies

Compiled by

### TERRI JOHNSON

Illustrated by

### DARLA DIXON

**BRAMLEY BOOKS**
www.bramleybooks.com

A Division of Knowledge Quest, Inc.
Gresham, Oregon

Published by BRAMLEY BOOKS
A Division of Knowledge Quest, Inc.
P.O. Box 474
Boring, OR 97009
www.knowledgequestmaps.com

Cover Design by Cathi Stevenson
Illustrations by Darla Dixon

Printed in the United States of America
Copyright © Terri Johnson, 2005
All rights reserved
ISBN # 1-932786-22-8

Publisher's Cataloging-in-Publication Data

Johnson, Teresa Lynn.
    What really happened during the Middle Ages: a collection of historical biographies / compiled by Terri Johnson; illustrated by Darla Dixon (What really happened... series, v.2).
        p. cm.
        ISBN 1-932786-22-8
Contents: Saint Patrick - Sower of Light in Ireland--Theodora - Empress of the New Roman Empire--Alcuin - The Man Who Loved Books--Good King Wenceslas - Duke of Bohemia--My Grandmother the Queen - Eleanor of Aquitaine--Joan of Arc - The Maid of France--Johann Gutenberg and the First Printed Book--Martin Luther Leader of the Reformation

1. Biography--Middle Ages, 500-1500. 2. Middle Ages. 3. Civilization, Medieval. 4. Women--History--Middle Ages, 500-1500. 5. Europe--History--476-1492--Biography. I. Dixon, Darla. II. Title. III. What really happened series.

CT114 .J64 2005
921--dc22                                                              2005933090

## Contributing Authors:

### Karla Akins
*Good King Wenceslas - Duke of Bohemia*

### Linda Crosby
*Joan of Arc - The Maid of France*

### Jennaya Dunlap
*St. Patrick - Sower of Light in Ireland*

### Kathleen L. Jacobs
*Martin Luther - Leader of the Reformation*

### Terri Johnson
*Theodora - Empress of the New Roman Empire*
*Johann Gutenberg and the First Printed Book*

### Francelle Somervell
*Alcuin - The Man Who Loved Books*

### Virginia Swarr Youmans
*My Grandmother, the Queen - Eleanor of Aquitaine*

*Other books in this series:*

What *Really* Happened During Ancient Times
*(scheduled for Spring 2006)*
What *Really* Happened During the Renaissance
*(scheduled for Fall 2006)*
What *Really* Happened in the Modern World
*(scheduled for Spring 2007)*

*e-books also available at*
*www.bramleybooks.com*

# TABLE OF CONTENTS

"Brevis a natura nobis vita data est; at memoria bene redditae vitae sempiterna."

"It is a brief period of life that is granted us by nature, but the memory of a well-spent life never dies."

**Marcus Tullius Cicero**, *Philippic 14.12*

"So teach us to number our days,
That we may gain a heart of wisdom."

**Psalm 90:12**, NKJV

# A Word from the Publisher:

Dear reader, young and old alike,

History is an interesting blend of facts, legends, assumptions and speculations. Historical research uncovers events from the past – how, when and where an incident happened. It cannot, however, fully explain motivations – why someone did what they did – or how an event can be interpreted so differently by two or more eye-witnesses. History is the story of people from the past – people who lived and died based on their convictions and perceptions about the world they lived in. *What Really Happened During the Middle Ages* is a compilation of stories based upon actual historical happenings. Some fictional elements have been added to contribute to the flow of the biographies. In the same way, some unsavory details have been left out or glossed over for the benefit of our younger readers and listeners. Dreams, visions and voices from heaven cannot be verified historically, but are integral aspects to some of the biographies in this book, as the characters themselves believed they were being guided by God or other heavenly beings. We hope that you will enjoy these historical tales of real live people and learn something new about the time period we call the Middle Ages.

*Terri Johnson*

*I dedicate this to my mother and dearest friend, Joy Marie Dunlap, who is also a published writer. She taught me to love writing in our home school, and has been the main source of encouragement and inspiration throughout my life and my journey as a writer. She is the one who introduced me to Saint Patrick, and instilled in me a love for history.*

# ST. PATRICK

## Sower of Light in Ireland

*by Jennaya Dunlap*

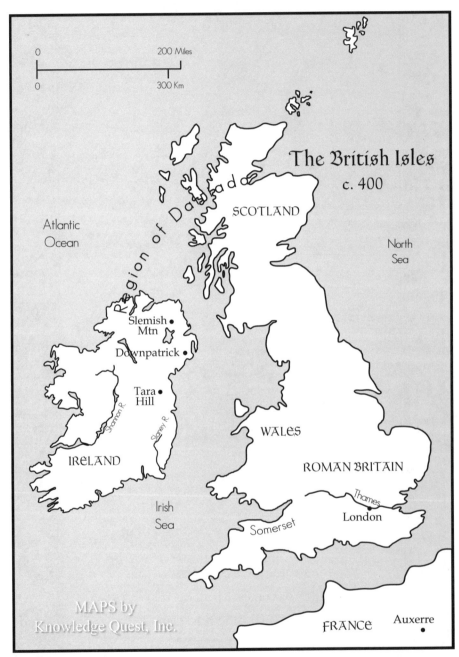

The British Isles
c. 400

0 _____ 200 Miles
0 _____ 300 Km

Atlantic
Ocean

Region of Dalriada

SCOTLAND

North
Sea

Slemish
Mtn

Downpatrick

Tara
Hill

Shannon R.

Slaney R.

WALES

IRELAND

ROMAN BRITAIN

Irish
Sea

Thames

London

Somerset

MAPS by
Knowledge Quest, Inc.

FRANCE

Auxerre

# 1

# ST. PATRICK

## Sower of Light in Ireland

### *By Jennaya Dunlap*

## The Land of Bondage

*Northern Ireland, around* 432AD

atrick's heartbeat quickened to the pace of his feet as every step took him closer to the palisade in Dalriada, Ireland. Memories, now nearly forty years old, of slavery under Miliucc, the cruel chieftain king who ruled the region, came back to him as he trod along the wooded trail. He had escaped long ago, and now he was coming back to buy his freedom, so he could walk the land a truly free man.

"What will they do to you?" Benen lifted anxious eyes to search Patrick's troubled face. This youthful son of another Irish chieftain was a new convert to Christianity, eager and loyal, but none of the trials that he had seen since he had joined Patrick could compare to the one that was coming.

"Be not afraid, Benen." Patrick put his arm around the

youth's shoulders as they walked. "God is with us and will protect us. This must be done in order for the Lord's work to be carried out unhindered."

Still, fearful thoughts pressed into his own mind. *They could kill you, Patrick. You are an escaped slave— by law you can be put to death. This is pure foolishness.*

The palisade was in view as they came out of the clearing. Patrick's heart pounded like the Irish war drums. Benen sung the words of the Lord's Prayer softly beside him, his voice shaky. Patrick drowned his thoughts in prayer— God had delivered them before and he prayed He would do it again.

As they approached the gates of the palisade, a strong odor of smoke met their noses. "Patrick, look! Smoke!" Benen halted and pointed, grabbing Patrick's attention. "It's coming from the center of the palisade! What could this mean?"

Patrick lifted his eyes and saw thick black smoke rising from Miliucc's fortress. Orange flames leapt from the walls, consuming them quickly. Bewildered, he stopped a young Irish slave who was fleeing from the fire. "What is the meaning of this fire?" he asked urgently.

"Master Miliucc heard that a former slave of his was coming, and he was afraid, and has gathered his possessions into his house with him and lit it on fire."

"But why?" Patrick's voice revealed his shock at the news.

"Because he heard that the slave was coming to convert him to his God," the slave told him, quivering. He turned and ran toward the woods.

"He could not bear to be converted, even in his old

age. He would rather die than be subjected to Christ's ways."
Patrick watched, dazed, as the flames licked at Miliucc's futile
earthly glory. As the choking, black smoke drifted toward
them, he fell to his knees, shaken. What was God showing
him now? His mind went back to that time so many years ago,
when he first became a slave....


# From Wealth to Slavery

*Slemish Mountain, Northern Ireland, around 395AD*

The sheep wandered about the beautiful green hillside,
grazing on the lush Irish grass. Patrick sat on the damp ground,
his staff lying beside him. His stomach was in a constant
turmoil from hunger and thirst, and the cold mountain air
aggravated the pain of the beating the head herdsman had
given him recently. It would be weeks now before he could
collect provisions down in the village.

Could it have been so few months ago that the sixteen-
year-old youth had sat at his father's banquet table in Somerset
of Roman Britain, dressed in finery and enjoying his parents'
wealthy position? He had grown up wealthy, with little
restraint, the son of a civil magistrate and tax collector. His
grandfather had taught him about Christianity, but he had
never taken it seriously.

All the pain of the past months came back as the
memories flooded him. The Irish raiders' boats, closing in to
the shore, the fire, killing and destruction that had suddenly
surrounded him as the warriors, armed with spears and

15

helmets, tore through the town, now unprotected since the Roman legions had fled the land...

Patrick could vividly remember the pounding in his heart as he ran through the streets, followed closely by his pagan pursuers. They were faster than he was, and soon he was bound with ropes and forced onto a waiting boat. He had known even then what awaited him in Ireland— slavery and all the horrors and drudgery that came with it.

He cringed even now, to think of the terrible treatment he had gotten on the way to the Irish shores, and on the journey to the northern kingdom of the cruel, warlike chieftain, Miliucc. He had been used to a life of ease and comfort, to the disdain and anger of the herdsman in whose charge he had been put. Many a time would Patrick be beaten for doing a job wrong or carelessly.

*I deserve this,* he had told himself. *I have sinned against God and rejected His ways.* The admonishing words of his Christian grandfather came to his mind in his despair, and he cried out to God aloud. "O Lord God, help me! Help me to repent and to follow Your ways! Give me strength in this hour of trials! Listen to my plea, O God!"

He had lain awake that night, under the stars, deep in prayer, as a new hope and faith came over him.

During the six long years of slavery that followed, he was beaten and mistreated as much as ever, but he found great solace in his walk with God. Throughout the cold days, spent with his sheep in the mountains, he prayed for hours at a time. He got up long before daybreak, even in the worst of weather, to continue praying and meditating on what he had learned.

One night, six years after the beginning of his enslavement, he had just gone to sleep on the mist-covered hill where he had been conversing with his Savior.

*Patrick!* His eyes flew open as he heard his name called in the darkness. He waited in silence for a moment, but nothing happened, and he drifted back to sleep. *Patrick!* The voice was distinct and urgent. As Patrick opened his eyes once more, a picture passed before his eyes— a ship sailing the open waters. *Come and see, for your ship is ready for you,* the voice spoke clearly.

He sat up straight and threw off his tattered cloak. This was the second vision telling him to return home. Perhaps it was now time to make his escape. He hurried up the path to the top of the hill, looking out over the quiet valley, and here he kneeled to pray, under the vast spread of the night sky.

The high, sweet call of a bird, fluttering about nearby, brought Patrick out of a light slumber with a start. He had fallen asleep, still on his knees. He stood for a moment in the pre-dawn cool, watching as the first streaks of light colored the distant horizon. In his heart he prayed still, asking for guidance. The first rays of sun shone on his face, lighting up the drops of dew on the grass. *Go now — it is time.* The moment had come.

Patrick quickly found his staff and the ragged bag of provisions that he had collected only yesterday, and he turned to leave.

## The Escape

Days of travel wearied Patrick, but the visions God had

given him came back to his mind to renew his courage. He crossed the mountains, avoiding roads and civilized areas lest he be discovered and recaptured. Mile after mile fell behind him, and at last he could smell the salt in the air. Gulls flew about above him with their mournful cries. He had reached the sea at last.

Dogs barked in the distance as Patrick approached the port. He pushed back his wind-whipped hair to catch a glimpse of the trading ship that was preparing to sail. His heart jumped, for it was the same ship he had seen so clearly in his vision! If he had had any doubts before that God's hand was guiding him, he entertained them no longer.

The excitement inside him grew as he drew nearer to the ship. The sailors busily tied up Irish hounds to carry onboard, to trade when the ship arrived in Britain. Two men looked up as Patrick came toward them, and one hurried to bring the captain.

The captain, a gruff man with wild hair pulled back in a sailor-style knot, stepped forward as Patrick reached them. "What is it you want, youth?" he asked roughly.

Patrick felt his heart pounding, but he spoke boldly. "My God has shown me in a vision that I am to go on this ship to Britain."

The captain and the sailors exchanged knowing looks and burst into laughter. "What will you pay us?" the captain demanded.

"I have the fare for passage, right here."

"But we do not want you or your God to get on this ship. You'll have to go elsewhere." The other sailors laughed roughly again.

"But God has shown me that I must go on *this* ship," Patrick answered calmly. "I'll kneel over there and pray for a while, to see if He will change your minds." With this he strode some distance away and knelt by a rock, as the waves moved in and out around him.

*You led me to this ship, O Lord. I know you won't fail me now. You can change the minds of these men.* Renewed confidence filled his heart as he prayed. Perhaps he should approach them once again to request passage. If this was God's plan, he could face the jeering and taunting.

Footsteps sounded in the shifting sand behind him. A sailor called out to him, several feet away. "The captain says we'll take you anyway. Hurry now — the tide is coming in."

"Thank you, Lord," Patrick said aloud as he followed the sailor back toward the ship. He boarded the ship in haste and was relieved when it set out quickly, for now there was no time for the men to change their minds.

For three days the ship traveled on the sea, blown by the gale that greeted them from further out. Patrick helped the sailors with their work but spent his free time in a solitary place, deep in prayer, while the pagan sailors drank and mocked him and his love for Christ. The captain particularly disdained his faith and mocked him mercilessly.

On the third day they had reached land, but it was not the English port at which they had intended to pull in. Wilderness covered the shoreline for as far as Patrick could see.

As they pulled the boat to shore on a sandy ledge, the sailors exchanged frightened looks. "We've landed in Gaul," one of them said. "Now we'll never reach Britain."

The men explored along the shore, looking for signs of civilization, but it was isolated and thickly forested, without a sign of other humans. The supplies on the ship grew scarce as days turned into weeks. The hungry sailors scoured the land for food, but with little success.

One morning, as they gathered wood to make a fire by the small shelter they had built, Patrick, as was his habit, retreated to the woods to pray. As the sun lit up the shore in dazzling orange light, he walked back toward the shelter. Even from a distance he could see the captain coming toward him.

His face held the same cruel, taunting look, but it was now mixed with anxiety and desperation. He stepped in front of Patrick. "What have you to say for yourself now, Christian? You boast that your God is all-powerful. We're starving to death, and we may not survive to sail back home."

"Nothing is impossible with God," Patrick answered him calmly. "Turn your heart to Him, and He will provide us with food for our journey." With this he knelt down again and beseeched God to bring them food.

He could still feel the sailors' disdainful glares as he stepped over to the fire to warm himself, but they were silent. There was no food, and the men, weakened from the lack of it, spent the morning close to the fire, arguing among themselves. Patrick stood up and turned to face the men.

"Before noon you will have food in great bounty. The Lord will have mercy on you." No one spoke, and for a moment the only sound was the crackling of the logs and the crashing of the waves on the nearby shore.

Patrick turned and walked toward the beach to spend some quiet time with God. The sun was nearly at its highest when he returned, with peace in his heart and renewed strength and confidence. He stepped quietly into the camp and sat down.

"Where is the food you promised?" a sailor asked. "Did your God give it to you at the beach?" A few laughed, but most of the men remained sober.

Patrick opened his mouth to speak, but a loud and continuous grunting grabbed the men's attention. Large numbers of pigs rushed down the hill from the woods, covering the path thickly and blocking the way into the forest. The sailors jumped up, grabbing their spears with joy.

Evening came, and the men were still busy. In spite of the abundance of food, they ate comparatively little, and even the amount they stored seemed little to Patrick. Much of the meat they sacrificed, burning it to honor their pagan gods. Patrick felt God's anger at the men for their ungratefulness, and he retreated to a dark corner of the ship to pray, while the men loaded it again.

## Beckoned to Return

Patrick tossed about on his bed, unable to sleep in spite of his weariness. His mind went over the travels of the last year, before he had arrived again on British shores. He had returned to his relatives and received a royal welcome. They had thrown a feast for him and heaped gifts upon him, yet somehow he did not feel content. He spent much time in prayer and now in reading the Bible, but God had not yet shown him what He wanted.

One night he drifted off to sleep at last, tired from another day of poring over his books, trying to make up for lost learning. A voice called his name, as clearly as in the vision in Ireland. *Patrick! Patrick!*

Before his eyes, he could see the people of Ireland, yearning for hope and light. A young man stepped forward from among them, carrying letters, as if from many of these people. One of these opened before him, so he could see the words on the page. "I am the voice of Ireland," it read. One person and another, and then everyone, cried out to him. "We beseech thee, holy youth, to return and walk among us again."

Tears flowed from his eyes, and he woke before he could read any further. He sat up, choked with emotion and tears. For hours he could not control them, and he prayed to God as he lay awake, begging Him to show him what His plans were.

Early in the morning he opened his books to study, but he could not bring himself to it. The words in the vision passed through his mind over and over, disturbing him greatly. He went through the day as if in a daze, and he was glad when night fell and he could rest.

As he slept, he again saw the Irish people, begging him to come among them again. He could hear their pleas, but he could not understand the words they spoke. Above it another voice spoke. "He that has laid down His life for thee, it is He that speaketh in thee."

He awoke with the words still flowing through his mind. A certainty came over him and he knew now that he must return to Ireland. Out his window, he could hear the first morning birds. He sat down by it and reached for the Scriptures on his table.

## Easter on Tara Hill

The wind stirred up Patrick's unkempt hair as he stood on the deck and gazed at the distant shore, still only a light speck on the far horizon. The ship rocked on the high waves as he held to the slimy rails. Ireland, at last, after so many years of waiting!

He had gone to a monastery in the town of Auxerre to study for the priesthood, not long after he had had his vision. But church politics had held him back from his calling for so long. Nearly forty years had passed since he had last set foot in the land where he had spent six years in slavery, and now he returned as a bishop.

Patrick met with opposition from the druids and chieftains nearly as soon as he set foot on Irish shores at the mouth of the Slaney River. The first man who showed interest in turning to Christianity committed suicide, and several times, for months at a time, druids and chieftains imprisoned him. The man who had been sent before him to be the bishop of Ireland had fled in terror, but Patrick stood his ground.

Benen, a chief's son, was one of his first converts. He listened with rapt attention as Patrick shared the message of the Gospel. When he had finished, Benen asked one question after another.

The next morning, as the sun rose slowly above the

horizon, spreading the sky with glorious colors, Patrick got up and awakened his companions, saying it was time to continue on their journey.

As they walked past the crude dwellings toward the hills beyond, Benen rushed toward them, his face alight in the dawn glow. He fell to his knees at Patrick's feet.

"Please allow me to come with you, Patrick, so I can learn more about this wonderful Jesus you told us about last night," he begged. "I want to serve Him, like you do."

Patrick looked at him seriously. "If you come with us you will face the same trials as we do. I will be able to spare you nothing of the hardships that may await us."

"You say that your God protects those who follow Him," Benen answered. "I'm not afraid — please let me come with you."

As he was talking to Patrick, the chief and other important men came and urged him to stay, lest his life be endangered. Benen refused and replied, "Nothing will sever me from this man whom God has chosen. I believe God wants me to go with him."

Patrick looked at the chieftain. "Allow him to have his way. He shall be heir to my sacred mission." At last the chieftain consented, and Benen set out with Patrick.

He became one of the most faithful Irish Christians, and he used his special gift for music to teach hymns and Psalms to new believers.

After discovering that Miliucc had committed suicide, Patrick headed toward Tara, where Loiguire, the high king, ruled, surrounded by his best druids. He arrived shortly before the night of the pagan Easter festival, when the high king annually lit a big bonfire and declared that light had returned to the earth at his command.

On that night, shortly before it came time for the king to light his bonfire, Patrick and his men gathered on a hill within sight of Tara and gathered wood to build their own bonfire in God's name. With trembling fingers, Patrick lit a torch and held it next to the heap of logs. In moments, flames caught onto the logs and spread, leaping high in the moonless sky. Benen started into a hymn, and soon they had joined hands around the bonfire, singing about Christ's resurrection.

In the palisade in Tara, King Loiguire raised the torch his druid handed to him, preparing to light the pagan bonfire. "Look," someone shouted, pointing toward the hill in the distance. "Another bonfire! Someone has already lit the first Easter bonfire!"

The king trembled with fear. Who would dare to defy the ancient pagan customs of the land? He called together his druid advisors, and one of them stepped forward with terror on his face. "O king, live forever. The prophecies of old times warn that if the fire is not put out this very night, it will spread throughout this land, and our traditions will be destroyed by the man who lit it and his coming kingdom."

"Never!" The king's face blackened with rage. "Prepare me twenty-seven chariots and gather all my druids and warriors together! We must confront and destroy this man!"

The horses, hitched to the chariots, tore through the Irish countryside, toward the hill where Patrick and his men added more logs to the fire, still singing. Patrick stood up, his heart trembling within him as he turned to face the angry men. His companions hung back in terror, all except Benen, who stood by his teacher's side.

Lochru, the king's highest druid, stepped forward to demand that Patrick put out the fire. His evil eyes were filled with hate as he insulted Patrick and his faith. Patrick waited calmly as arrogant words were tossed upon him, but when Lochru heaped slanderous insults on his precious Lord, he stepped forward, anger warming his heart.

His eyes, gleaming with God's light and presence, met the druid's in a steady gaze. Forgetting his fears, he shouted out in a powerful voice, "O Lord, You can do all things, and You have sent me here to spread Your Word. May this evil man who blasphemes You and Your Holy Name be picked up and die through Your power!"

He stood in silence, surprised by his own boldness. Suddenly, Lochru was catapulted in the air and fell back onto the ground with great force. A warrior bent over him. "He's dead!" he shouted.

The king glared angrily at Patrick. "Seize him and kill him!" he cried out, pointing. Fearfully, the warriors turned toward Patrick.

The boldness in Patrick's heart did not die out. "May God arise and His enemies be scattered!" he declared. Confusion and chaos followed, as the earth began to shake. Horses spooked and galloped away, leaving the king's men stranded as the chariots twisted and broke.

The king trembled as he fell to his knees, his eyes filled with a mixture of anger and fear. His men knelt too, while

Patrick thanked God aloud for His deliverance.

King Loiguire never did become a Christian, but his opposition slowly died out as his fear of God's power grew. Several of his sons and daughters and some of his men were converted, however, and the way opened for Patrick's work.

## Missionary to the Irish

Ireland at that time was made up of many small kingdoms, each with its own king or chieftain, for towns did not yet exist in the country. They fiercely guarded their pagan ways and were hostile to Patrick's missionary efforts. Some of the kings were converted and often the people in the kingdom followed suit, but this was not always the case. Those who became Christians sometimes allowed their sons to travel with him, to be taught by him, in honor of an ancient custom. He usually brought gifts to the kings, in return for the freedom to spread the Gospel in their lands.

One day he was traveling on a lonely road in one of these kingdoms, having paid the king in full. Benen was with him, and so were many other people, some of them converts and others asking eager questions about Christianity. They pulled with them a cart with all their belongings.

Suddenly, a thunder of hoofbeats pounded toward them on the road behind them. The travelers turned to look, and their hearts thumped with horror. The king's warriors were approaching speedily on horseback, armed with spears and other weapons. The king himself rode between them.

Some of the people who were with Patrick fled, but he and his faithful companions stood fearlessly on the road. The horses snorted and reared as they were pulled to a stop nearby, and the warriors jumped off, their spears drawn.

"What is it you want with me?" Patrick confronted the king in a calm, clear voice. "I have paid all that you asked for, and you granted me your consent to start a mission in this kingdom."

"I changed my mind — you came to destroy our old ways and replace them with your worthless religion!" the king shouted. He turned to his warriors. "Seize this man and his companions, and kill them."

The warriors grabbed Patrick's arms and held them in an iron grip, preparing to kill him. Patrick cried out aloud to God. "Oh my God, You have created this earth and everything in it. Save us in this hour of death, for You have shown me that You have more for me to do on earth."

The king's bloodshot eyes filled with rage, but the hands that held his reins trembled. At his orders, the armed men seized hold of the cart and took the bags from the travelers' shoulders, making off with them. Patrick's arms and legs were tied back and bound with iron, along with those of his companions. They were dragged to a dark jailhouse near the king's dwelling.

Patrick fell to his knees in the darkness. He thanked God for his life and beseeched Him to guard over them still and help them to be freed.

He spent two weeks in prison before some dear friends, probably Irish converts, convinced the king to let him and his men go. Patrick stepped into the sunlight again and thanked God for His intervention, as he looked around once more at the rich green hills of his adopted country. His belongings were returned, and, once more, he gathered his friends and companions and went on his way.

God blessed him and prospered his mission, and many hardworking Irish in kingdoms all over turned to Christ. Patrick baptized them and continued to teach them. When he had made many converts in one kingdom, he left a trusted Irish Christian in charge of teaching and helping them and went on to the next province or kingdom.

Remembering the miserable years of his own slavery, he fought against the slave trade in Ireland and eventually succeeded in abolishing it entirely, but not before many long years of perseverance. He was the first known person to speak out against slavery, at a time when almost no one saw anything wrong with the cruel practice.

Little did he know that the next slaveholders he would confront would be not from Ireland, but from Wales, another part of the British Isles.

## Coroticus

Hoofbeats clattered on loose rocks in the Irish hills beyond the site of the new church, where new converts were at work raising the stone walls and preparing to lay the rafters. Patrick set down the heavy stones he had in his arms, turning to see what the other men were watching. The rider tore toward them at a frenzied speed, his head bent forward with concentration.

Patrick hurried down the hill with a pounding heart. It could only be bad tidings that this man, a young priest whom he had discipled for years, from a nearby coastal kingdom, had come to convey. He offered a steadying hand as the man slid from the horse's bare back, sweating and out of breath.

"What brings you here, brother?" Patrick asked anxiously, offering the man water from the heavy jug.

"Terrible—terrible news," the man gasped out between heavy breaths.

"Tell me, what has happened?"

"A Welsh warlord, Coroticus, and his men— they raided our kingdom as I was conducting baptisms for new converts." He paused, his eyes full of anguish and anger. "They have killed so many of our men, and they have taken the women and children as slaves. I escaped, and so did a few others, but they have wrought so much death and destruction!"

"How dare they do such an evil deed— and they call themselves Christians. They blaspheme against God's Name! Where have they gone?"

"Back toward the coast," the priest told him. "Patrick, we must do something! We cannot let them get away with this!"

Patrick fell to his knees and prayed aloud. He wept openly about the vicious attack on these new children of God. What should he do? As he prayed, suddenly he knew what must be done.

"Take several of my trusted presbyters with you, and go after them. Beseech them to let these converts go, and report to me what they say. May God be with you and help your words to prevail."

It was not long before they returned, weary and frustrated. Coroticus and his men had only jeered at the presbyters and did not listen to their pleas. Patrick went into the house where he was staying and wrote a letter of excommunication to Coroticus and the men who had carried out his cruel orders, so that no Christians would associate with them.

The letter explained what they had done in patient detail, condemning it with great indignation. Even though he was the bishop of Ireland, and not of Wales, he felt that it was the only way to prevent more such raids, but it caused resentment among the people who read it in Britain.

## Rest at Last

By the year 457AD, Patrick had worked among the Irish for twenty-five years. We don't know exactly how old he was by then, but he was probably somewhere in his seventies. Tired and worn-out, he returned to Downpatrick, the place where he had first arrived on Irish shores, so many years ago, and there he lived for the last few years of his life.

He died on March 17, around 460AD, though the exact year of his death is still disputed. The Ireland he saw when he first arrived there as a slave and the country it was at the time of his death were vastly different.

Christianity now had a firm hold on the Irish nation. Patrick had founded 300 churches in kingdoms across the country and brought more than 120,000 people to Christ. Irish slavery had ended, and so had human sacrifices, and women and the very poor were no longer so downtrodden. And the writings from Europe that he had preserved survived throughout the Dark Ages, when much of the wisdom people had gained up to that time was lost in this time of hardship and ignorance.

Seeing all that he had accomplished, it is easy to understand why Ireland still cherishes him in memory, celebrating St. Patrick's Day on March 17th every year in honor of him.

*About the author:*

Jennaya Rose Dunlap wrote this story at the age of 15. Jennaya, now 16, is home schooled and the editor of a magazine for home schooled girls, ages 8 to 18, *Roses In God's Garden*, published by LightHome Ministries, www.lighthome.net. She is also the author of *Against All Odds*, a researched historical novel set in World  War II Poland under Nazi occupation, published as a serial story in her magazine. Jennaya enjoys writing and researching, drawing, singing, playing violin, horseback riding, and discovering Eastern European folk songs on the Internet. She enjoys spending time with her family on their acre beside a meadow with a mountain view, in California.

*To my parents, who taught me that I could accomplish anything I desired, but that it was my heart and dedication to a task that truly mattered.*

*And to Todd, my dear husband and best friend, who encourages me daily and supports me wholeheartedly in my endeavors.*

*Authors note:*

Theodora became the empress of the Byzantine Empire in 527AD at the age of 27. This empire stemmed from the ancient Roman Empire which began in 753BC and fell in 476AD to the many barbarian kings who swept through the region. The eastern half of the Roman Empire, however, managed to hold strong against the invaders at their borders and maintained their government for nearly a thousand years during the Middle Ages. These Byzantine people never thought of themselves as "Byzantines", only as Romans. And so they are referred to as such in this story. It was not until the 17th century that French scholar DuCange coined the term *Byzantine* after the former name of the Empire's capital city, Byzantium. The town's name was changed to Constantinople by the Emperor Constantine I in 324AD.

# THEODORA

## Empress of the New Roman Empire

*by Terri Johnson*

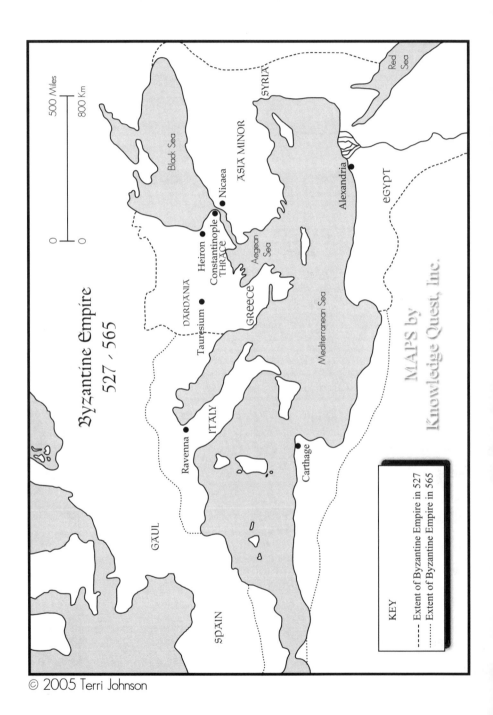

Byzantine Empire
527 - 565

KEY
----- Extent of Byzantine Empire in 527
······ Extent of Byzantine Empire in 565

MAPS by
Knowledge Quest, Inc.

500 Miles

800 Km

Black Sea

Nicaea

ASIA MINOR

SYRIA

Red Sea

Alexandria

EGYPT

Heiron

Constantinople
THRACE

Aegean Sea

DARDANIA

Tauresium

GREECE

Mediterranean Sea

Ravenna

ITALY

Carthage

GAUL

SPAIN

© 2005 Terri Johnson

# 2

# THEODORA

## Empress of the New Roman Empire

*By Terri Johnson*

### The City Ablaze

She stood in the shadows of the alcove, quietly looking out the window upon the burning city. She could see the flames licking the walls of the new church tower and burning portions of the palace and nearby courtyard. She touched the cold stone at the window's edge. Cold now, but for how long? She could hear the angry voices of the people outside. They shouted, "Nika! Nika!" (the Greek word meaning *victory*) and banged on the palace gates.

Theodora shuddered. She reached down and lifted the skittish cat at her feet. She stroked its fur gently, soothing its frayed nerves. "Oh Eudoxia," she whispered to her cat, "What should we do now?"

She stepped back from the window and leaned against

the hard stone wall listening to the sound of her rapid heart pounding in her chest. She had only a few minutes more to think and to pray before she must speak with the Emperor, her husband.

Even now, the tenth day of the riot, the people outside were raising their angry fists and shouting, demanding that she and her husband, Justinian, step down from their thrones and no longer rule the Roman Empire. They wanted a new emperor to take his place.

*What advice should she give?* Theodora wondered. Should they stay and face this angry mob? Could they possibly win back their confidence and trust? Or should they run away – far from this chaos and into the quiet countryside beyond?

Still stroking the nervous cat, she remembered that it was Zeno who 50 years before had faced this same situation. The people of Constantinople no longer wanted him as their emperor. He escaped from the city and hid in a small village for two years before returning to reclaim his throne. *We could do the same*, thought Theodora.

She and Justinian could slip out of the palace under the cover of night. Of course, they must not ride in the emperor's golden chariot nor could they wear their royal garments of purple cloth as these things would surely attract attention. Disguised in servants' clothing, they could exit secretly through the East Gate which opened to the Bosporus, the waterway leading to the Sea of Marmara. They could take a boat until they were safely away from Constantinople and then journey by land to Tauresium in the region of Dardania, where Justinian was born. Once there, they could live quietly until this whole matter had passed.

Or they could stay.

Theodora put down the frightened cat and wrapped her cloak more tightly about her small shoulders. Hurriedly and quietly, she walked down the long corridor to the adjoining Daphne Palace. As she listened to the haunting echoes of her footsteps on the mosaic floor, she was once again amazed to think that she was the Empress of this vast empire and that their future and very lives depended on this decision and on the advice that she would give her husband. It was all beyond her wildest childhood imaginations…

## The Bear-Trainer's Daughter

Theodora grew up in this city of Constantinople, but on the other side of town. She was born the second of three daughters in the year 500AD. Her parents were entertainers – her mother an actress and her father a bear trainer. Their lives centered around the Hippodrome, the huge arena for entertainment in the middle of the city. The Hippodrome hosted chariot races, plays and various circus-type performances.

There were two clubs that organized the events held in the Hippodrome. They were called the Blues and the Greens. They were like two separate teams who strongly opposed and disliked each other. Theodora's father, Acacius, worked for the Greens. When Theodora was very young, probably four or five, Acacius became ill and died. Theodora's mother was devastated and wondered how she would take care of her three little girls with no husband and no job.

She remarried quickly and asked the Greens if her new husband could have her former husband's job as bear-trainer. They coldly replied, "No." In a desperate attempt to gain back the job, Theodora's mother braided flowers into her girls' hair and led them in a procession out to the middle of the Hippodrome arena. With hands outstretched, as her mother instructed, Theodora looked into the faces of the hundred thousand on-lookers as her mother pleaded for the bear-trainer's job for her new husband. She explained that her sweet daughters would go hungry without the money the job would provide. The Greens simply laughed and waved them away. Theodora was crushed. She was acting humble and demure just as her mother had wanted and yet she had not won the approval of the crowd. Then the leader of the Blues called out that he could take the job as their bear-trainer. Theodora's heart soared. When she looked up, the Blues were standing on their feet and clapping and cheering and wishing them well with their smiles. Theodora would be a devoted Blue fan for the rest of her life.

Theodora was fond of her new father. She enjoyed helping him care for the bears that he trained for his circus acts. She especially loved to feed them from her hand. When she could, she played with the other children whose parents worked at the Hippodrome. The long summer days could be sweltering if a breeze didn't kick up from the Black Sea to the east or the Aegean Sea to the west. On these hot days, when their chores were done, the three sisters and their friends would chase each other through the public fountain at the entrance to the Hippodrome. But the days of her childhood could not last forever.

By the time Theodora was twelve, she was performing herself. She was a talented actress, particularly in mime – acting without words. She never forgot her earlier experience in front of this crowd and she was determined to become the best and most convincing actress on the stage. Her heart swelled with pride when she could make her audiences laugh or cry out loud. The people loved her, throwing flowers and even money to her. She helped to take care of her family with the money that she earned. She thought that she would probably be an actress for her entire life. She had no reason to believe otherwise.

## Chance Meetings

When she became an adult, she began to travel about the region, visiting some of the cities and villages that were part of the eastern Roman Empire. One day, she arrived in Alexandria in far-away Egypt, where her life was to dramatically change. She knew that she was searching for something and yet she could not put her finger on it. She had an emptiness in her heart and soul that had not yet been filled. She felt unloved and unworthy and wished to make a better life for herself. It was here in Alexandria that she found what she was looking for. One day, she entered a magnificent church and fell down on her knees before the altar. A priest by the name of Timothy reached down to her and shared with her the love of God. It was on that day that she became a Christian and decided to dedicate herself to helping the poor and the helpless. She remained in Alexandria for more than a year, learning all that she could from the church leaders there, especially Timothy whom she called her spiritual father. Soon, however, she realized that it was time to go home.

When she was back in Constantinople, she decided that being an actress would not be a fitting occupation for a good Christian woman. So, she took the job of a wool-spinner in the marketplace.

One day, while she was spinning a batch of sheep's wool into yarn, she heard the blare of trumpets and a man's voice calling out, "Make way for the heir to the throne!" She looked up from her work as an army regiment was passing by. There she saw Justinian, the Emperor's nephew, for the first time. But this was not the first time he had seen her. Many years before, he had seen her on the stage and had always hoped that one day they would meet. He thought that she was the most beautiful and determined woman he had ever seen.

He dismounted from his horse and asked her name. With a polite bow, she replied, "Theodora." In the days and weeks that followed, he came by often. Soon he asked Theodora to become his wife and she said yes.

Their wedding was dazzling and elegant, befitting the ceremony for the Emperor and Empress to be. Attended by her ladies-in-waiting, Theodora walked regally down the aisle, dressed in the purest of white and royal purple, her magnificent jet black hair framing her stunning face. Nearly everyone believed that Justinian had chosen a delightful and deserving bride.

Following the weeks and months of their wedding, Justinian proved his love and admiration for her by consulting her in all matters, including his most important decisions regarding the governing of the Empire. He found her to be extremely intelligent and practical in her advice. And she showed her love for him by deferring to him in most decisions and respecting his natural-born instincts of compassion and understanding. She became his true partner in life and would prove to be an invaluable asset when the Empire fell completely on his shoulders.

They were not married long when Justinian's uncle died, leaving the throne to them. They rode down the streets of Constantinople in the Emperor's golden chariot to the Hippodrome. And there Justinian was crowned the Emperor and Theodora the Empress of the eastern Roman Empire. As she looked out into the crowd, she recognized the people and they remembered her. Only this time she was not standing before them as a little girl to beseech their help, nor as an actress to entertain them, but rather as their queen to rule them. And once again, they cheered her and threw flowers at her feet.

## Fortunes Change

This adoration of the people did not last long. Her husband, Justinian, made some decisions early in his reign that angered many people. His overriding desire was to expand the Empire to its former glory and to do this he needed a larger army and more money. He decided to acquire more funds by raising the taxes on all the people in the Empire, but especially on the wealthy landowners. He sent out a man by the name of John the Cappadocian into the countryside to collect the money. The wealthy landowners became angry at the high taxes, and the poor farmers who could not pay them sold their farms and moved to the city to look for jobs. Constantinople became over-crowded with homeless and hungry families looking for work. Resentment was building against the Emperor Justinian at this time in his reign.

Another decision Justinian made which angered many citizens was that he told his senators he no longer needed their advice in running the Empire. For hundreds of years, senators had been offering their emperors advice whether they chose to accept it or not. They were outraged that he did not even want to hear the advice they had to offer anymore.

One day, as emotions were running high in Constantinople, a fight broke out in the Hippodrome. Some people were killed in the fighting. The mayor of the city, Eudaemon, decided that two men should be hanged after they were tried and found guilty of murder. Strangely, on the day of their execution, they both fell through the noose and landed on the ground unharmed. So the executioner tried again and the same thing happened. Two priests in the crowd, who felt this was surely a sign from God, grabbed the two stunned men and ushered them to their church for safety. The police ran through the streets to the church and waited outside for them to come out so that they could be arrested once again. Interestingly, one of the convicts was a Green and the other one a Blue.

Two days later was the Ides of January, a popular chariot

racing day in Constantinople and the Emperor and Empress were expected to attend. When they were seated in the royal viewing box, the two leaders of the Blues and Greens stood side by side and addressed the Emperor. "O' Emperor," they called in unison, "We beseech you to let our two captives go." Justinian remained silent and waited for the racing to begin. At the conclusion of each race, the leaders would again stand together and ask the Emperor to release the prisoners held in the church. Each time he remained silent. Then someone shouted out, "Long live the Blues and the Greens!" Never before had the two groups bonded together in a single cause and the strength of the statement caused the entire assembly to respond in chorus, "Long live the Blues and Greens!"

Justinian became frightened by their solidarity and determination as they rose up in strength against him. Hastily, he and Theodora escaped through the special palace entrance and back to the safety of the Imperial Palace. On their retreat down the spiral stairway, they could hear the angry yells of the people echoing in the empty corridor. "Nika, Nika!" the people shouted as the bronze door slammed shut behind them.

## The Nika Revolt

...Theodora arrived shortly at the Daphne Palace where she found her husband surrounded by his most faithful and trusted friends and advisors. The room was hushed as no one knew quite what to say. The situation appeared hopeless. Ten days had now passed and the vicious mob would not be appeased. Yesterday, Justinian not only freed the two men hiding in the church, but he fired the two with whom the people were most angry – John of Cappadocia, the tax collector, and Eudaemon, the mayor who tried to have the two criminals hung for their punishment. These actions were too little too late, according to the mob. They continued to demand that Justinian and Theodora step down and give up their crowns.

Finally, Belasarius, the captain of the royal army, spoke up. "We can easily steal the two of you out of the city and to safety. You can then come back when the tensions have died down."

With looks of resignation, the men began to discuss the details of their plan for escape. Suddenly, Theodora stood and a hush fell across the room.

She stepped before Justinian's advisors and spoke these words, "My lords, the present occasion is too serious to allow me to follow the convention that a woman should not speak in the counsel of men. Those whose interests are threatened by extreme danger should think only of the wisest course of action, not of conventions. Now in my opinion, in the present crisis, if ever, flight is not the right course, even if it should bring us to safety. It is impossible for a man, once he has been born into this world, not to die; but for one who has reigned it is intolerable to be exiled. May I never be deprived of this purple robe, and may I never see the day when those who meet me do not call me 'Empress'." And turning to Justinian, she continued by saying, "If you wish to save yourself, my Lord, there is no difficulty. Over there is the sea and there too are the ships. Yet reflect for a moment whether, when you have once escaped to a place of security, you will not prefer death to such safety. I agree with an old saying that the purple is a fair winding sheet (burial shroud)." After these words, she nodded respectfully to the men and resumed her seat.

Justinian and the other men looked sheepish for she had a courage that surpassed theirs. And he knew that she was right – that it was better to die trying to regain the Empire than to live in humiliation for the rest of their lives.

He took her advice and sent Belasarius with his army as well as his own palace guards to the Hippodrome to quell and quiet the rebellion. Many men died that day as had many in the ten days that had come before, for which Justinian and Theodora were exceedingly sorry.

They humbly and bravely returned to the Hippodrome to declare that the Revolt had come to an end and that it was time to rebuild the city. Justinian made many changes from that day forward to better please his subjects. And Theodora began to take an even larger share in running the government after that day. In fact, the people considered themselves to be ruled by a dual headship instead of a monarchy as Theodora had as much a hand in the affairs of state as Justinian. Some would argue even more so. And Justinian knew that he would not be the Emperor of the Roman world if it were not for Theodora. He would be grateful to her for the rest of his life.


## The Benevolent Queen

In the years immediately following the Nika Revolt, as it

came to be known, Theodora began to travel again. This time, however, she traveled for pleasure, not in pursuit of a better life. Her favorite destination was Heiron – a quaint town to the north. Here she had a beautiful palace with splendid gardens – its colors vibrant against the green backdrop of the countryside.

When she would set out from Constantinople, she would adorn her royal headdress, wear her costly jewelry and ride in a carriage covered with a purple silk canopy pulled by pure white horses. She would be attended by hundreds of palace guards, musicians and ladies-in-waiting. Her traveling procession was indeed an impressive sight to behold.

The grandeur and power of the Empress and Emperor were becoming ingrained upon the minds of their subjects. Certainly now, no one believed that they could easily be removed from power. The sincerity and determination of Justinian, along with the pomp and splendor of Theodora were putting their leadership of the Roman Empire on a more solid footing.

Now that her authority was no longer in question, Theodora set out to accomplish what she had vowed to do so many years before – help the helpless, especially those who were being unjustly treated by others. She turned two of her palaces in Constantinople into shelters for such mistreated individuals. One palace became a retreat for priests and monks who were in need of shelter and protection. She was especially drawn to helping the clergy as she never forgot the kindness of her spiritual fathers who loved a frightened girl who had found herself in Egypt, friendless and fraught with shame. She was eternally grateful for their compassion and she loved and cared

DIXON 2005

for these shepherds of the faith until her dying days.

She also used a magnificent palace as a home for actresses and other entertainers from the Hippodrome who were desperate to change their lives for the better. She knew their hard life first hand and she was determined to help them in any way she could, offering both physical care for their bodies and spiritual care for their souls.

Ironically, one day she was able to offer care to the very person she loved most in this world.


## The End is Near


The unthinkable happened. Justinian became ill with the ghastly Bubonic Plague. Most of the people who contracted this disease died from it and whole towns and villages were being wiped out by its deadly effects. Theodora spent endless hours by her husband's side, wiping his brow with a cool cloth and giving him sips of water to drink. Justinian remained sick for weeks and during the daylight hours, Theodora had to run the government without him. The world had turned upside down as people were dying everywhere and she was there to provide calm direction to the chaos in the streets. Each evening, she would return to her husband's side and whisper the words she needed him to hear, "You will live, my love. It is too soon to say good-bye."

In time, Justinian began to recover and the deadly plague and its destruction passed through the region and into other kingdoms and realms. The people began to put the pieces of their lives back together, what was left of them. Everyone had lost someone and the mourning was great. Theodora was relieved that she still had her family, for Justinian was all that she had. Sadly, they never had any children together, as much as they had hoped they would. Now that Justinian's life was spared, she knew that it was time to tell him that her life would not last much longer. She did not have the sickness from the plague, but she knew that she was becoming weaker and that her time was running out.

One can only imagine when and how Theodora broke the news to Justinian about her illness. It must have been very difficult for him to bear, for when she died of cancer on the 28th of June in the year of 548AD, he grieved the loss of his beloved wife whole-heartedly. The court was shut down and a state funeral of magnificence took place.

Mourners filed into the Imperial Palace to pay their last respects to Theodora, Empress of the Roman Empire. Lit by the glow of hundreds of candles and dressed in royal purple with a golden crown upon her brow, the Empress looked like a fairy-tale princess awaiting an enchanted kiss to bring her forth once more. But the parting kiss of her prince Justinian only sealed the truth more firmly that indeed Theodora had departed this world to join her true King in the next.

The body of Theodora was placed upon a funeral bier and on it she made her final journey to the church where she had worshipped for nearly 30 years. The people of Constantinople flocked about her to get a parting glimpse of their queen. They crowded the streets, they leaned dangerously out of their windows and they stood on the rooftops – all in an effort to say good-bye to their Empress Theodora.

Upon her arrival at the church, the priest called out in a booming voice for all to hear, "Go Forth, O Empress! The King of Kings and the Lord of Lords calleth thee home."

Justinian burst into uncontrollable sobs. When he in time regained control over his heavy heart, he bravely announced, "My wife, who loved me in this world is now praying for me in the next."

## Afterword

Justinian lived another 17 years after the death of his beloved Theodora, but he never forgot nor failed to champion her causes. In her absence, he became a faithful supporter of the religious leaders whom Theodora vowed to protect and he always made shelter available for actresses seeking a better life. In the truest sense, Theodora lived on in the life of her devoted husband.

The eastern half of the Roman world, now known as the Byzantine Empire, continued for nearly a thousand years and remained a strong and powerful society. It produced many great rulers and thinkers, men and women alike. Theodora, the bear-keeper's daughter who rose to become Empress, is certainly counted among them.

*About the Author:*

Terri Johnson is the creator of Knowledge Quest maps and timelines (www.knowle dgequestmaps.com).  Her mission for the company is to help make the teaching and learning of history and geography enjoyable for both teacher and students. She has created and published over 15 map and timeline products. Her *Blackline Maps of World History* have been widely recommended in the education community and published in *The Story of the World* history series by Susan Wise Bauer. Terri and Knowledge Quest recently won the "Excellence in Education" award granted by The Old Schoolhouse magazine for best geography company of 2003 and 2004. Terri resides in Gresham, Oregon with her husband Todd and their four children whom she teaches at home. She is expecting baby number five any day now...

*This story is dedicated to my children because they cannot imagine a world without books. We have all benefited from Alcuin's legacy.*

# ALCUIN

## The Man Who Loved Books

*by Francelle Somervell*

York

North Sea

ENGLAND

SAXONY

POLAND

• Cologne

• Aachen *or*
Aix-la-
Chapelle

Prague

BRITTANY

BOHEMIA

The Empire
of Charlemagne
c. 800

FRANCE

Tours •

BURGUNDY

Venice

BULGARIA

Parma •

GASCONY

PROVENCE

LOMBARDY

EMIRATE OF
CORDOVA

Rome

Mediterranean Sea

MAPS by
Knowledge Quest, Inc.

AFRICA

# 3

# ALCUIN

## The Man Who Loved Books

*By Francelle Somervell*

### The Journey Home

*On the road to Parma, Italy,* 781AD

"Ah, my poor old bones," said the man to himself as he trudged along the dusty road. "I'm much too old to be making a journey like this." He stopped and peered down the lonely road, hoping to see the town in the distance. No, only the winding ribbon of a dirt path was before him. He shook his head and continued to talk to himself, "To see that great city, Rome, it was a glorious blessing, but with every blessing comes the work. And for me, it is the work of returning home."

A few travellers were on the road with him. Travel was discouraged for all people unless one was a pilgrim, or an official on court business. The rulers of the land believed that too much travel upset the society and encouraged a shiftless people. In fact, the Frankish King, Charlemagne, wanted to keep the road clear of what he believed to be vagrants and wayfarers. He wanted people to remain on the land.

So then, on this lonely stretch of road, near the town of Parma, Italy, the old man walked alongside his fellow pilgrims, returning from the city of Rome. For some, their journey would be over when they walked into the streets of Parma. For others, like himself, their journey would continue until they crossed the sea and returned to the green Isle of Britain. The old man sighed at the thought of his long journey home and wished he were home now, in the halls of the cathedral school in York.

He loved his life's work because it allowed him to be surrounded by the companions of his life: his treasured and rare books. He breathed in deeply and closed his eyes as he thought of the treasures contained in the library at school. Holy books and books written from the great Greek and Roman thinkers of hundreds of years ago stood like soldiers at attention in the library in York. He patted his bag, reassuring himself of the two books travelling with him.

*Two treasures*, he thought, *two precious and wondrous treasures*. They were worth more gold than what the common peasant could ever hope to see in ten lifetimes, maybe even twenty.

He thought of the long and tedious hours of copy work to produce just one book. The copyist would sit, hunched over a desk, meticulously forming each character in order to produce a single book. However, there was no other way to create a new book.

To think of a book being lost or destroyed was an evil the old man could not even ponder, as he clucked his tongue in dismay. He wondered, not for the first time, how many precious volumes of the great classical writers from ancient Rome or Greece had been lost to mankind forever, irretrievably lost, like gold dust scattered into the wind, blowing away a priceless treasure. He shuttered at the senseless waste and pulled his cloak in tighter to his chest, against the invisible wind.

Of course his main reason for travelling to Rome had been to see the Pontiff, the ruler of the Church. To see and to speak with the Head of the Church was an honor indeed. Very few men of his acquaintance could boast of the experience. He was a privileged man indeed. However, once he had completed his audience with the Pope, he had gone about the task of obtaining a book or two while he was on the continent. To have traveled months on his pilgrimage to Rome and not use the opportunity to collect a precious book or two was unthinkable. His love of books would not allow it.

His school's library in York was perhaps the greatest in all of Britain. The library made the school the center of learning for Britain, a place where those who were blessed with the ability to read could glean from the past thinkers of the world.

The old man had lived at the school for more years than he cared to remember. He had been blessed to be born into a high ranking family. When he was old enough, he had entered the school as a pupil in Archbishop Ecgberht's school. At the school, he had marvelled at the mystery of seeing the written characters on the soft parchment slowly transform from senseless scratches and scribbles into letters, and then into words! Once he had understood the individual words, he had begun to understand that the words were ordered together to create ideas! It was a mystery indeed.

His love of learning had made him decide to remain at the school after his studies had been completed. He loved teaching. Now, at the ripe old age of fifty, he was the headmaster. He became the headmaster three years ago, in the year of our Lord, 778. It was a privilege to lead and direct the studies of the young men and he was able to travel about, in search of new books for the library.

Thinking of his journey brought his thoughts back to his precious books, lovingly packed away in his travelling bag. He sighed once again and thought of his aching feet. He wondered when he would arrive in Parma. *Soon, I hope*, he thought, as he looked down the long and winding road.

## An Invitation from the King

The man's feet throbbed as he sat down with a thump on the three-legged stool. He would have sat by the fire but it was too crowded. He did not want to lower his old bones to the floor, for fear of needing assistance to return to a standing position. He was thankful to be inside, out of the elements. He could hear the murmurings of the people in the large hall. They were whispering in an excited manner. Evidently, some great and important person was due to arrive today. The old man simply shrugged his shoulders as he smiled to himself. Since he had seen the most important man in the civilised world, all others seemed to lose their imminence. He was more concerned with trying to find something to eat. At the thought of food, his stomach produced a loud, grumbling sound.

At the same moment, the din of the crowd rose in pitch and the old man turned his head to see the object of commotion. A noble had entered the hall. He was a youngish man, though not a green youth, thought the old man. He must be a man of some importance, even though he was dressed in rough clothes, more suitable for a day of hunting rather than impressing his fellow noblemen.

Servants rushed about, bringing some ale made from barley to the young man. Just then, the old man heard the name of this nobleman. Here, in the same hall, was the great king of the Franks, Charles the Great. He was known by many names, depending on the speaker. To the Franks, he was Charlemagne. He was Karl der Grosse to the Germans, and to the Spaniards, he was known as Carlomagno. Whatever the name, they all meant the same: Charles the Great.

He had ascended the throne after his older brother's death, ten years ago. In the space of just ten short years, he had conquered many lands. He roamed his dominion, travelling from palace to palace and now, here he was, in Parma, Italy. The old man wondered why this young ruler was in Italy.

As he returned his thoughts to the food before him, the young ruler approached his table and sat down.

"So, I hear you are a scholar, sir," said Charlemagne to the old man. The old man smiled, "Yes, your majesty, so some say that I am."

"What is your name?"

"My name is Alcuin," said the old man. "I am the head master of a school in York. Perhaps you have heard of it. It is Archbishop Ecgberht's school." With those words, Alcuin bowed his head in humble service to the Frankish king.

"So, then, you must be a man of great learning. You must be well-read, as well as well-travelled," said Charlemagne as his eyes assessed Alcuin's road-weary garments. At that moment, a servant brought the king a platter of boiled meat and set it before the ruler.

"Bah! You think this meat is fit for a king?" demanded Charlemagne. "I will not eat this meat. Take it away and prepare me some meat that has been roasted over a fire," as he waved the food away.

He turned to Alcuin and continued his questioning of the scholar. Alcuin privately thought that boiled meat was better than no meat but he supposed that if one was a king, he could afford to be picky about his food. For Alcuin, his food consisted of bread. Bread made of rye, or wheat, or barley. If he was blessed, he might enjoy some soup made with root vegetables to soften the crust for his old teeth. Meat was a luxury, eaten only if the hunters had snared some game in the woods. The domestic animals were more useful alive, too precious to be eaten. Besides, the poor animals were overworked and underfed, not unlike most people, he thought. Underfed, overworked animals made for very tough eating, and Alcuin wondered if his poor old jaw was not quite up to the difficult task of chewing tough meat. No, he would be thankful for his simple barley loaf and some vegetable broth.

"I hear that you have acquired a magnificent library at this school of yours in York. Is this fact true or just a wishful rumor?" asked Charlemagne, interrupting Alcuin's thoughts.

"Yes, your majesty. I can attest to the truth of what you have heard. I have spent many years gathering books from around the known world. It is one of my life's most satisfying achievements."

"So, you believe books have value?" asked the young man. Alcuin nearly choked on his bread.

"Yes, I believe in the value of the written word," he replied. He looked into the ruler's eyes and continued, "It is like the wealth of a hundred kings." Alcuin shifted his gaze to the fire as he continued, "And to know how to read and write, I would not have a king's ransom in its stead." He turned and faced Charlemagne.

"Why do you ask?" questioned Alcuin. Charlemagne pushed his body away from the table and stood, pacing the floor.

"I ask because I, too, believe in the power of knowledge. But knowledge is not like gold. One does not simply go and dig until one has found a vein of precious metal." He paused and turned to Alcuin, his eyes blazing, "This reading and writing, it is a mystery to me. But I would have my court officials and my sons know how to read and write." He sat down and moved his chair closer to Alcuin.

"But I have a problem. It seems as though people do not believe me. They do not value some activity that does not produce something that can be seen, or touched. All around me, people scoff at learning." He shook his finger at Alcuin, "But they are wrong! Learning has much value."

Alcuin's heart began to beat quickly. To hear his own passion being voiced by this powerful ruler was incredible.

This man before him had the power to change the course of history.

"Come to Aachen," said Charlemagne. "Come and work with some scholars that I have called together. Let us change the course of my kingdom."

## The Lost Art of Learning

Alcuin sat at his desk, the warm glow of the candle flickering on the plaster wall. It was cold. Ah, one of the less glorious aspects of being a scholar, he said to himself. All this time spent, hunched over a parchment and sitting in a cold room. The cold would touch his hands and feet, slowly creeping up his limbs until his entire body would be so cold that he could hardly hold his quill.

And his eyes! Trying to read this illegible writing, it was God's mercy that he was not already blind from the long hours squinting at the black scratches and scrawls. All these letters and words ran together, until they began to swim and shimmer on the page. He sighed to himself. Perhaps he should think about trying to create a better script. Clear and concise lettering was needed. It would certainly help his fellow scholars in their pursuit of reading and copying the great works of the masters. *Mmm...*, he thought. Could he actually accomplish such a worthy feat?

He picked up the parchment he had been studying. His eyes ached and he rubbed his temple, trying to push the pain away from him. The script was written in the Merovingian style of writing. Not only was the script impossibly messy, the

Latin was vulgar and barbarous. Did not anyone know how to read and write classical Latin? He sighed once again. So much had been lost with the fall of the Roman Empire. The entire continent had descended into ignorance and darkness. To be sure, the Romans had their own vulgar ways and habits that Alcuin was glad to see pass away. However, with the decline of the Empire, came the decline of learning. No longer were there schools where young men could be taught. Basic reading and writing skills were no longer acquired by the nobles. And, of course, the result was ignorance. Most noble-born young men were ignorant, unable to contribute to the workings of civil government. No wonder the great king, Charlemagne wanted to see some reform. Alcuin clicked his tongue and shook his head. Yes, there was much work to be done.

And the clergy were not much better! All around him, Alcuin was surrounded by unlearned and ignorant men who could neither read nor write basic Latin. Bah! The Latin that was spoken by most people was a vulgar excuse for Latin. It was a poor representation of the beautiful language. And how, he asked himself, could the clergy pass on the great truths of the Faith, if they could not even read or write themselves? It was a shame. Learning had passed down into the abyss.

He stood up and paced the small room. Alcuin promised himself that he would not lose heart. Did not God Himself bring him into Charlemagne's court? Did not God Himself speak the word and the world was created? Yes. The Almighty valued words and Alcuin would not lose heart. There was much work to be done.

Pushing the Stone Uphill

The two young men came into to the small room, laughing and pushing at one another. Their cheeks were ruddy from the cold wind outside. They were about to enter into a full-blown wrestling match when they heard a loud "humph." Immediately, they straightened their shoulders and bowed their heads towards their master.

"Our apologies, dear sir. We were busy with our other duties," said the younger one.

"Bah," said Alcuin. "I know what those duties are." He stood up from his stool and walked towards them.

"Duties like hunting and sword-play?" he asked.

"Yes, master," they replied in unison.

"Young sirs. I do not have anything against those most worthy pursuits. I only ask that you attend to your lessons in a timely manner and you give these lessons the honour they are due." He cleared his throat before he continued.

"He who does not learn when he is young, does not teach when he is old." He stared at the wall behind the two youths. "Do you know why this statement may be true, young sirs?" The two young men shuffled their feet and stared at the floor.

"Because they have no worthy thoughts stored within the confines of their minds," he said as he knocked on their heads, startling the youths.

"Attend to your lessons!"

Alcuin directed the young men to their stools and instructed them to take out the parchment they were meant to

be studying. He sighed quietly. It felt like he was pushing up the same stone that had been Sisyphus' doom. Every day, he was pushing against the crude nature of the unlearned, trying to ignite within their hearts the desire to learn. To instill in these young men the ability to read and write when they did not see the worth of learning was a near impossible task.

Most noblemen scoffed at the thought of reading. To most noble-born men, it was a skill less valued than woman's work. They wanted to see their young sons excel in manly skills. Skills like hunting and sword-play. Alcuin did not want to discourage these manly arts; he only wanted to broaden their feeble minds so that they could contribute to the workings of the Frankish society. Unlearned men did not contribute to the development of a better society. It was Charlemagne's dream to raise the people he governed to loftier heights.

However, if these young men did not see the value of basic learning, how would they ever contribute more to society than a strong arm? Alcuin was thankful he had the full support of the Frankish king. Otherwise, he would be sorely tempted to pack up his bags and return to York.

As he thought of his beloved country, he closed his eyes and saw the gentle, rolling green hills, dotted with sheep. And, of course he thought of his beloved library, filled with precious works. Charlemagne had charged Alcuin to build up a new library. Charlemagne wanted to build up a library that would rival the great cathedral library in York. His goal was to build the greatest library in the continent.

Well, thought Alcuin, great goals required great work. He straightened his back and turned towards his students.

Gathering together a great library needed scholars capable enough to be sent around the known world with enough ability to copy books. And before they could accomplish such a great task, they needed to be able to read and write in classical Latin. He looked up at the young men waiting for him to begin. There was much work to be done.

## Reviving the Trivium

Alcuin was busy thinking. He was busy thinking how he might develop a suitable course of study that was modeled after the Roman system. It was a good system, he thought to himself. It covered all the basics that a young man might need to contribute to civil service within Charlemagne's court, or should he desire, to enter into the clergy to further the work of the Faith on the earth.

Under the Roman Empire, there were public schools for the citizens. These schools employed men called *rhetors*. These *rhetors* were paid out of the Roman Empire's treasury. This use of public money ensured the future of an educated group of men to enter into civil service, and thus, the continuation of the Roman Empire.

All of which brought Alcuin back to the present. Charlemagne's first objective for Alcuin, and the other scholars gathered here at Aachen, was to promote a competency in written Latin among the clergy. Alcuin shook his head. Even amongst the clergy, who were supposed to be somewhat educated, there was a shocking level of ignorance. To find a man among the clergy who could read and write classical Latin was like finding a needle in a haystack. One could look and look for a long time and still not be guaranteed of finding it.

So then, Alcuin's first goal was to create a working syllabus to be used for the basis for clerical education. He thought back to the Roman system based on the seven arts of learning. They consisted of the literary arts called the *trivium*. The subjects within the *trivium* were grammar, rhetoric, and dialectic. Grammar was simple enough. He could use the works of classical Latin grammarians like Prisian and Donatus. If he could accomplish a fluency in Latin amongst the clergy, he would be greatly pleased. Unfortunately, there was more to becoming a learned man than knowing the basics of reading and parsing Latin verbs, which brought his thoughts to the other aspects of the *trivium*.

Rhetoric involved the art of persuasion. In Athens, when democracy was at its height, every citizen was expected to contribute within the political arena and the ability to argue his case was considered a necessity. Of course, as autocracy grew, the voice of the public was lessened. Now, the need to be skilled in rhetoric was not as highly valued.

Then there was the study of dialectic. It was concerned with the skill of formal logic. The purpose of studying dialectic was to instruct the young man how to gather evidence and how to apply the rules of induction to solve a problem. It was a very profitable skill. *Did we not all come across problems which needed to be solved?* asked Alcuin to himself. Yes, he would use his books by Aristotle and the commentaries by faithful Boethius.

In contrast to the literary arts, the other subjects in the ancient Roman curriculum were formed around the *quadrivium*.

These subjects were based around mathematics. There was arithmetic, which Alcuin found difficult due to the use of those clumsy Roman numerals. Then there was geometry. Alcuin would use Euclid to study geometry.

Next was astronomy. The study of astronomy consisted of a mixture of mathematics and some chronology. A bit strange, Alcuin thought, but useful nonetheless. Finally, there was the study of music. Music was the study of questions in relation to all the musical notes upon the scale. He was fascinated by the mathematical basis of harmony. Yes, the study of music was a noteworthy subject.

However, all these subjects, however noteworthy they were, would be no use to students, if they did not value learning. Simplicity was needed. Alcuin needed to devise a syllabus which was simple enough to be managed, but thorough enough to provide a sound foundation of learning. He concluded he should focus on the basics. He would concentrate on grammar and rhetoric, teaching his students how to compose both prose and verse in Latin so they would truly be fluent and accurate in written and classical Latin. It was worthy goal, considering the times.

## The Making of Parchment

"Teacher!" called out a young man to Alcuin as he was walking across the courtyard. Walking toward him was one of his students. He wondered what the youth needed. Alcuin had left his young scholars for the morning, instructing them to complete various tasks while he had spent a very pleasant morning visiting his friends who lived and worked in the palace.

Wherever Alcuin went, he would strike up a conversation, introduce a riddle, or simply speak a kind word to those around him. He had just come from visiting his friend, the royal seneschal. It was always a pleasing way to spend the morning in the bake-house or the kitchen, laughing and talking with the seneschal. And, of course, Alcuin was sure to enjoy a bit of freshly baked bread during his visit. However, it seemed as though duty was pressing upon him. He turned towards the young voice.

"Yes, young sir?"

"We are out of parchment," he said as he shuffled his feet in the dirt.

"Well, it is not the first time, nor, I suppose, will it be the last time," replied Alcuin. "Come, lad. Let us go and see what is delaying our parchment."

The pair walked towards a small building near the outer wall of the palace. Outside were two young boys stirring large, iron cauldrons, boiling over with its chalky liquid.

"Ah," said Alcuin. "It looks as though they are trying their best to provide us with our needed parchment." By the cauldrons, three hides lay neatly stacked, ready to be soaked in the chalky water. Alcuin was not sure if the animal hides came from sheep or goats as the hair had already been cut from the hide, to be made into something useful. Nothing was ever wasted within the palace grounds.

One of the boys bent over and picked up one of the hides. Carefully, he dropped the hide into the hot water. Soon the air would be filled with the unpleasant smell of wet wool. Alcuin wrinkled his nose in distaste and hoped he could find an excuse to leave soon.

"Ah, Alcuin! Come and watch us at our labours. Take note of the effort that goes into preparing your precious parchment," said a man who was overseeing the boys at the cauldrons.

"Good Louis," hailed Alcuin. "I give you thanks for providing us with our much needed parchment."

"I confess," said Louis. "I do not see the need for so much parchment. How many books should one ever want to read? Surely one book would be enough for most men."

"Ah, Louis," cried Alcuin. "The riches to be found in books are worth more than you can ever imagine! Trust me when I say, we need more parchment," he said as he patted Louis on the shoulders.

Louis sighed, thinking Alcuin was perhaps a bit crazy but he valued his friendship and remembered how Alcuin always had a kind word or a smile.

"Come, then," Louis said. "Let us see what is happening to your parchment," as he motioned Alcuin to follow him into a small shed.

Alcuin followed Louis into the shed. He blinked his eyes to adjust to the darkened room. After a moment, he could see the frames which held the boiled skins. Each frame held a whole hide. The frame's purpose was to hold the hide taut so that a young boy could scrape the hair off the skin. Each boy had a small piece of pumice, which he would use to smooth the skin and rub away the hair. Alcuin marvelled at the thought of pumice. *How could a stone weigh no more than a wad of cloth?* he wondered. The mysteries of the earth!

As he watched the young boys working with the hides, he stepped closer for a better look. It was tedious work. The boys had to be careful not to damage the precious skin. To kill a sheep or a goat that could have kept on producing wool was wasteful to most people. The hide could be made into a garment, or some shoes; anything more useful than parchment.

Sheep and goats were scarce and they were needed to produce wool. Parchment was seen as an unnecessary luxury. All these factors contributed to the shortage of parchment.

Once again, Alcuin wished for a change in the hearts of the noble born men. Reading was a necessary skill. He sighed and shook his head. He could only fulfill his own calling and leave the rest to God.

He turned his attention to the workers. They were working carefully on the hides. There was not much room for error as the boy would gently rub the hair away. After the skin was smooth, the skins would be pressed down and flattened. Once the hides were flat and dry, they could be cut into useable sheets, ready to be written on.

Alcuin ran his fingers along the scraped skin. He could still feel hair on the skin. It was nearly impossible to rub off all of the hair from the skin. It made for difficult copy work, writing over the hairy stubble. Of course, the parchment produced at Aachen was of a fine quality but he had certainly come across some shocking samples of parchment. Many times, he had heard the complaints of copyists, moaning about the difficulty of writing upon hairy parchment. Perhaps it would do the copyists some good to see the work that went into the preparing of parchment.

Alcuin turned to Louis and said, "Your work is much appreciated, Louis. I see that much effort goes into each sheet of parchment." Next, Alcuin turned to his young scholar, "See here young man and give thanks for your parchment." The young man nodded and smiled.

"Yes, sir," said the youth. He looked around the shed and then continued, "May we take a sheet or two?" he asked. "We are working on the copy of Ovid that you borrowed from Tours. We do not have enough parchment to finish the task." Alcuin patted his shoulders and turned to Louis.

"Louis, do you suppose that one sheet of parchment might be ready for this young lad?" Louis shook his head sadly.

"No, my friend. It will be at least another week before the hides are dry enough to be cut into sheets. I beg your patience," he said.

"Ah, good Louis," said Alcuin. "We will be patient." He turned to his young student and said, "Come, friend. Let us come away from these good workers. We will have to make due with washing out some other parchment."

He bade Louis good day and walked away, taking a deep breath of fresh air, free from the smell of wet wool.

"But Alcuin,' said the student. "I thought that you could not abide by the practice of washing out parchment."

Alcuin sighed, "Yes, it is true. However, one must be practical. This book we are copying from the monastery in Tours must be completed soon. We do not want an incomplete copy for Charlemagne's library."

The boy was right. Alcuin did not like the practice of washing away words, even if the old words were making way for new words. He was secretly afraid that many books had disappeared forever and the thought made him sad. However, he was also a practical man. He would do what was needed to finish the job. He would find some obscure parchment that did not have anything of importance written on it and he would wash away the ink, making room for new words.

"Come lad," said Alcuin, motioning the boy to walk faster. "Let us be about our business."

## In the Classroom

Alcuin had lived at Aachen for a few years. He enjoyed his life here, living near the Frankish king. In fact, he believed that he could even say that he had the privilege of calling the king his friend. If not for Charlemagne's support in the pursuit of learning, Alcuin would have found his employment at the palace most difficult. He even had the pleasure of instructing some of Charlemagne's sons. Once again, Alcuin gave thanks for the enjoyment of his life's work.

He was expecting some students soon. The young men came from various backgrounds. Today, Alcuin would be working with Raban Maul and a few others. Just then, the young men burst into the room. Raban Maul was followed by other students. One young man was a Frank, his father one of Charlemagne's nobles while the other was a Saxon. Alcuin smiled as the young men sat down.

"Welcome, young sirs. I trust you are ready to apply

yourself to learning today, young Maurus."

The young man returned the smile and replied, "Yes, sir Flaccus."

Alcuin chuckled to himself. He had the habit of giving his students nicknames, based on literary works or from names of students from past teachers. For young Raban Maur, he had named him Maurus, after the favorite pupil of Saint Benedict.

He, himself, had taken on the nickname of Flaccus. Alcuin felt a connection between himself and the scholar from long ago. He had taken up the name because of Flaccus' love of learning. In fact, Flaccus had once written, "I loathe the uneducated man in the street and keep him at a distance." Alcuin chuckled to himself. If he followed dear Flaccus' example, he would live a lonely life. However, he could aspire to learning and to lead others along the golden path as well.

He turned his gaze towards his students. "Come now, young men. Let us be about our work." He looked at the young Saxon.

"*Doctrina sed vim promovet in sitam,*" said Alcuin. The young man stammered and looked down at the floor.

"Speak up. Does this statement confuse you? You must apply yourself to your Latin, young sir." He walked around his desk and stepped towards the Saxon.

"It means *Instruction enlarges the natural powers of the mind.*" Alcuin smiled to himself as he looked at this young man, struggling with the intricacies of Latin verbs. These young men had burst into the thicket of grammar and needed to be instructed in the mysteries of number, gender, case and tense. Ah, the complexities of Latin grammar, he thought to himself.

He patted the youth on his shoulders and exhorted him to study more diligently.

He had devised a method of instruction based on the dialogue method. It involved a simple question and answer form, between student and teacher. He turned and began to instruct these young men.

"What is man like?" he asked Maurus.

"An apple on a tree," Maurus replied.

"Well done, young man." He turned to the other youth. "What is his state?"

"That of a lantern in the wind," replied the Frankish lad.

"I see you are applying yourself to your Latin. Well done."

Alcuin continued his questions for the remainder of the morning, helping these young men as they laboured through their Latin studies. He was thankful that he could fulfill his life's calling.

## Alcuin Writes a Letter

Alcuin was bent over his desk, writing one of his many letters. He loved writing letters. Besides learning and teaching, letter writing was one of his most favorite past-times. He had retired from his duties in Charlemagne's court last year. He had begun to feel the weight of his age and had longed for a gentler pace of life. Charlemagne had arranged for Alcuin to become the abbot at one of the finest monasteries in Gaul. He now lived at St. Martin in Tours. Alcuin enjoyed the new life, even if he did sometimes miss the palace splendour. And of course,

Charlemagne's new palace at Aix-la-Chapelle was a sight to behold! He smiled to himself as he thought of young Einhard, one of his former students. Einhard had designed the palace. He was proud of his former pupil's achievement.

He returned his thoughts to his letter. Presently, he was writing to his friend in York. He wanted to send some of the young copyists to York and bring back some books he had collected while living in York. He wrote:

*My dear friend,*

*I would ask that you would be so kind as to send to us some of your beautiful books so that we might plant them in the minds of our students, just as a seed, or perhaps like a flower. I promise to you that I will care for them, so that they, too, might produce beauty and fruit here in France.*

He was tired. He rubbed his eyes and put down his crow feather quill. He was certain the abbot in York would agree to his request. He felt an urgency to bring some of those books to France. With all of the Viking invasions, one could not be certain if those books would be safe in Britain. He shuddered at the thought of the destruction in York in Lindisfarne, Northcumbria. When the Vikings came, they destroyed everything, including books. He would feel much better when he held those rare books in his own hands.

He leaned over and snuffed out the candle. It was time for sleep, for there was still much work to be done.

## Epilogue

Alcuin died in 804AD, just four years after Charlemagne was crowned Holy Roman Emperor. Considering the times, he lived a long and full life. He had many accomplishments in his life but the most important one was the development of the new script, called Carolingian minuscule. This script was clear and easy to read, unlike its messy precursor, called Merovingian script. This older script simply ran the words and sentences together, making reading a difficult chore.

Another major accomplishment was his work of restoring classical Latin to a literary language. The "vulgar" Latin that he speaks of in the book is the beginnings of the French language. In fact, as the decline of the Roman Empire progressed and the learning of Latin with it, all the people who had previously spoken Latin, developed their own unique versions of the language. Therefore, Latin is the parent of all the romance languages in Europe such as French, Italian, and Spanish.

Alcuin was right to be worried about the possibility of a Viking invasion in York. The library in York grew more famous and collected more books for many years after Alcuin's death. However, in 866AD, the Danish Vikings attacked York, destroying Alcuin's beloved library. One can only wonder at such a loss of so many books.

For the modern reader, we find it difficult to conceive of a time when books were rare. Alcuin lived in a time when life was a struggle to survive. The production of goods barely managed to feed and clothe the people and a surplus of anything was rare. Thus, to use a skin for anything other than the necessities of life must have seemed wasteful or frivolous.

We will allow Alcuin himself to sum up his life, as written in his own poem, *Epitaph*.

Alcuin was my name: learning I loved.

*About the author:*

Francelle currently lives in New Zealand with her New Zealand-born husband and four children. She enjoys outdoor pursuits such as hiking, camping and walking along the beach, something she can do easily since the coastline is only a 90-minute drive from any point of the country. She enjoys indoor pursuits such  as quilting and reading, along with writing. She earned her BA in English through Massey University in New Zealand and would like to continue writing. She is currently working on both a novel and a picture book for children.

*I dedicate this to my Lord and Savior, Jesus Christ, and to my darling husband, Edward, who has never failed to believe in and love me.*

# GOOD KING WENCESLAS

## Duke of Bohemia

*by Karla Akins*

KEY

**Budec** - location of first latin school
**Levy Hradec** - location of the first Christian Church in Bohemia, St. Clement
**Stara-Boleslav** - location of Wenceslas' murder.
**Stochov** - location of the oak tree
**Tetin** - location of Princess Ludmilla's Castle

© 2005 Terri Johnson

# 4

# GOOD KING WENCESLAS

## Duke of Bohemia

### 907 - 935 A.D.

*By Karla Akins*

now fell in tiny flakes and the wind blew as soft as a baby's breathing. Glistening wisps of sparkling white crystals danced around the tops of the trees. It was St. Stephen's Day in Prague, the day after Christmas. A crowd had gathered at the square to gawk and point at the sight before them. Some shouted, others whispered, and many ran to and fro, waiting for a chance to bid on their favorite item for sale.

"I'll give ye this pelt of otter and a bottle of mead for that lad there," a rickety little man with matted, gray whiskers shouted.

A young lad named Viktor sat on the ground in front of him trembling. His face was pale and his lips were chapped. Tears stung his cheeks in the cold winter air. He was tied to a post in the middle of the square, surrounded by other young boys, girls, and women, all bound to one another with leather straps. Each of them sat on the ground with sad, tear-stained faces in front of a large, raucous crowd.

Viktor was for sale and he was scared. His father had died two weeks before and now he and his mother were to be sold as slaves to people from the Middle East and Africa. He sure hoped they would buy his mother along with him. He could not bear to be without her, and he knew she was more scared than he.

"This fine lad is worth a good sight more than that lousy pelt of yours and your stinking mead." The slave trader, a large, muscle-bound man with lustrous umber skin turned to Viktor. "Stand up boy," he sneered. Viktor stood and the slave trader ripped the thin tunic from his body. "See here?" he said to the little man pulling at his grimy beard, "This lad is healthy as an ox, and not a spot nor scar on 'im. Never a broken bone, and," the man looked through Viktor's curly locks of blond hair, "no lice, neither. He'll make the finest slave in your master's house!"

The man pulled again on his whiskers, squinted his eyes and looked over at his mother. The trader knew good and well slaves weren't nearly as valuable as cattle, and healthy or not, he was not going to pay more than a few pelts to get one of those puny slaves for his master.

"What about that wench there?" he nodded toward Viktor's mother, Ivana. "She's been hangin' on to the lad since the beginnin'. He her boy?"

"Aye," the slave trader said. "But she's not as strong as he is. Look at how scrawny she be." The slave trader lifted his mother's chin and his mother stared blankly back at him.

"Looks addled to me, and not too smart."

"She's smart enough!" the boy yelled, struggling to get free. "She goes where I go!"

"Aye, a feisty one I see," said the bearded man. "Okay, ye got yerself a deal. Two pelts and a half-bottle a mead."

"Ye give me one of them auroch pelts, a knife and three bottles of mead and ye got yerself a deal," the slave trader said sternly. "He be a lusty, healthy lad, with a lot of years ahead of 'im."

A voice came up from the crowd: "I crave your pardon! I'll do ye better! I've two pelts of auroch, three swans, a blackbird pie and one skein of wine to give ye in exchange for the lad and his tunic!"

"Sold!" the trader said immediately, turning toward the familiar voice. It was that crazy Duke of Bohemia again, come to fetch another boy.

"And the maiden too!" the Duke shouted.

"The maiden too, aye," the trader said. "I doubt I can trade her elsewhere for such a fine price."

The man with the whiskers scowled and walked on, studying the other children and women for sale. That boy and his mother weren't worth what the Duke had paid, and it was more than he could afford today anyway.

The Duke gave the slave trader all that he had bid, and then walked over to Viktor and his mother with a twinkle in his eyes and a smile on his lips. Viktor looked into the face of the Duke as he untied the straps on his wrists. He wondered what fate had in store for him now. The Duke went toward his mother to untie her.

"Don't touch my mother!" he screamed. He was too afraid to jump on the Duke's back to stop him, even if he wasn't tied up, but he wanted to.

The Duke looked up at the young lad and smiled gently as he untied the ropes around his mother's wrists.

"Relax, lad," he said gently. "I will not harm your mother." Then he reached toward the boy and touched his shoulder. "Nor you. I am here to help you – not harm you."

He finished untying their feet and gave them each a crust of bread from his pocket.

"Thank you," the boy and his mother whispered, grateful for the bread and freedom from their bonds.

"Come hither," the duke said. "Follow me. We have but a short journey to the castle for more bread — and pottage as well. And then, lad, we'll find ye a new tunic."

Viktor's mother looked at him, frightened, but he tried to act brave for her. He was the man of the house now, and it was up to him to take care of her – even if they had no house of their own anymore.

"It's okay, Mum, the gods be watchin' that be sure. I said extra prayers today."

His mother nodded hopefully and they followed the kind Duke through the forest uphill to Prague castle. It was a long walk and the winter wind, though soft, was biting. Viktor was shivering, and the kind Duke put his cloak about his trembling shoulders.

"Anon you will be sitting in front of Katiana's fire, drinking warm milk and eating swan pie," he said. "Perchance a good washing down is in yer future – I could smell ye from miles away!"

The Duke threw his head back and laughed at his own joke. Something inside of Viktor told him he didn't need to be afraid of this kind man. But he was still afraid. He sniffed at himself. He smelled just fine. The Duke must smell something else.

"What are ye going to do with us?" Viktor asked boldly, trying not to let his chin quiver.

"What do you suppose I should do with ye?" the Duke asked, his eyes twinkling.

"Let us go home," Viktor said.

"Pray thee, lad, what happened to cause ye to be standing in the slave trader's square?" the Duke asked gently.

"My father, a worthy and skilled candle maker was attacked by a wild boar," the boy said. "No matter how hard we prayed to the gods, the attack of the boar made his leg sick and he died. He couldn't do the candle making, and we couldn't pay our debts, so we were sold by our debtors to pay what we owe."

The Duke nodded. It was a common story these days. He hated seeing the children tied like animals to beams in the middle of Prague each week. The Arabs from the Middle East had an insatiable appetite for white slaves from Bohemia,[1] but not if he could help it. He bought as many children as he could each week. If only he could buy them all.

"Verily, young lad, tonight ye be not a slave. Tonight, ye be a guest of the Duke of Bohemia for the feast of St. Stephen's.

---

[1] Now Czechoslovakia

Ye and yer mother will dine at his table and eat his food. But not until ye get a new tunic!"

"Is the Duke a nice man?" Viktor asked meekly. "He doesn't eat children and their mothers does he?"

The Duke threw back his head and laughed.

"Nay, he won't be found eating children, lad. Ye won't be the Duke's dinner this night." The Duke laughed loud and his voice echoed among the trees and fell like eiderdown into the freshly fallen snow. Ahead was the grand castle. Soon they would be at the bridge to cross the moat and then they would be inside. Viktor's stomach rumbled impatiently. His toes were numb and his ears ached from the cold. He had never eaten swan pie. He could hardly wait.


"Ouch! I pray thee, stay! Stop it! Mercy!" Viktor wiggled and pulled away from the large, bulbous woman wiping at his face and ears.

"Settle down, Lad! I can't clean ye when you're wigglin' so!"

When Viktor and his mother had arrived at the castle, they were ushered into an enormous kitchen, where servants bustled about plucking geese, pheasants, swans and a various assortment of other fowl. Mutton and pork were basting on spits, and bakers were kneading dark dough and baking breads. Other servants were decorating scrumptious meats, already roasted, to make them look as they did before butchering. One young lassie carefully placed a pheasant's feathers back into the succulently roasted bird. Viktor's nose nearly burst with joy at the variety of delicious scents — aromas his nose had never before experienced or relished.

In front of a giant hearth — bigger than the cottage he and his mother had lived in before his father died — blazed the hottest fire Viktor had ever seen or felt. The woman washing him poured a pot of hot water over Viktor's head and he howled even louder.

"Mama! Mama!" he cried. "Help!"

He had never taken a bath in his life! His mother had told him to never get wet. It could mean getting sick – and to get sick with even a cough could bring certain death. So why was his mother allowing this woman to do this to him? He was terrified and annoyed. He did *not* like the feeling of that hot water in his ears!

He wiped furiously at his eyes and opened them only to find his mother giggling with a young girl Viktor's age. She was helping his mother put on a fresh tunic. Another girl was combing his mother's hair. What was going on? Why was his mother giggling like that, and why didn't she help him?

"The Duke deserves ye to be clean at his table, Lad," the big woman named Katianna said. The more he wiggled the harder the woman scrubbed so he decided it would be better to stand still. But it wasn't easy. This was his first bath – and he didn't like it one bit!

"It will be okay, Viktor," his mother spoke softly through her giggles. "I think we are safe now." Then she began to cry. His mother had not acted like her real self ever since his father died. He could hardly figure her out these days. For so long she had taken care of him – but now he felt he needed to take care of her.

"Pray tell — the duke — what is he like?"  Viktor asked as the woman put a clean tunic over his head and helped put his arms through the holes.

"The Duke is the finest man in all Bohemia," Katianna said. "He is kindly, good and generous."

"Aye, that he is," one of the young servant girls said. "And a Christian, too."

"A Christian?  What is that?" Viktor asked.

"It's a long story," Katianna said. "But, since it will take a while longer for the swans to roast — perhaps I can tell you.  Do you like stories?" she asked.

Viktor nodded eagerly.

"Well, then, if ye sit very still and let me clean yer toes – I'll tell ye the story of our good Duke Wenceslas."

Viktor loved stories almost as much as he loved bread, so he sat on a stool and plopped his foot onto Katianna's fluffy lap as she sat across from him.  Her lap was soft as a pillow and he liked the sound of her smooth liquid voice as she spoke.  Her cheeks were scarlet and her eyes shone with happiness in the reflection of the fire.  He was feeling sleepy, but he fought to keep his eyes open by staring at her round cheerful face.  He wanted to hear the entire story.

"Long ago, there were three beautiful sisters that ruled Bohemia.  They were the daughters of Pace, the prince who started a school that taught religion, hymns, prophecy and magic.  In those days, there was no writing, so the princesses had to memorize everything.  In those days, magic was the highest form of learning."

"And it is, indeed," Viktor said, his eyes wide with attention.

"Says who?" asked Katianna, grimacing at the young man's dirty feet.

"Why, says anyone ye ask, of course," he said.

"Well, it's not what the Duke would say, were ye to ask him," one of the young girls named Dora said. "So don't be sayin' so at his table."

Viktor crinkled his brow. *Why on earth would anyone not think that magic was the most important thing there was?* He looked at the lady cleaning his feet as she began again to speak.

"When the sisters' father died, he had no sons, only his three beautiful daughters to take rule. There was Kazi, who used herbs and magic incantations to heal the sick. There was also Teta who was a pagan priestess, and Libuse a very wise pagan prophetess.

"The wise and beautiful Libuse ruled as a judge along with twelve of the wisest men in the realm. They sat under that Linden tree ye passed when ye came here. You know, the big fat, tall one with the gnarled arms?"

"Aye," he said. "I saw that tree. Tis ugly and old it be."

"Aye," she said. "That be the one. And holy it was in those days for 'tis where people married and worshipped the goddess, Freya."

The lad nodded. He knew of that goddess, and all the others he and his mother worshipped.

"One day, when Libuse was judging an argument between two brothers, she decided in favor of the younger, and the older was made furious. He began to shout and bellow, 'Why do we men listen to a woman when we all know women have no brains!?'"

"Have they none?" Viktor asked. He really didn't know. All his life he had been told women and children were worth less than cattle – perhaps it was a lack of brains that made it so.

The big woman slapped his leg with a thick hand. "Nay! They have as many brains as any man, and don't ye be forgettin' it!"

The women all laughed and Viktor rubbed his leg. It burned a little where the woman had slapped him, even though she had done it playfully.

"When the pretty and wise Duchess Libuse heard this, and saw that the crowd did not come to her defense, she said, 'Yes, I rule like a woman with kindness and mercy. But you think this means I'm weak. You want a harder, crueler ruler? Then your wish shall be granted.'"

"She sent for her sisters and they talked all night long. Then, she went into her secret garden and fell before the gold and wooden idol, Perun, who had a head of silver and a beard of gold.

"A few days later, a meeting was held between all the leaders of the clans. Every man wondered if he would be chosen as the husband of Libuse.

"'You did not appreciate your freedom while I was your ruler,' she told them. 'So I shall no longer be your ruler. Instead, my husband will rule you. He will demand the best of your herds and children for taxes whenever he feels like it and you will pay dearly for it. Would you like to choose my husband for me, or would you like my advice?' the Duchess

Libuse asked.

"'Advise us!' shouted the crowd. So the Duchess Libuse rose and with a far-away look in her eyes said to them, 'Go to the small stream called Bilina, and to the little village of Stadice. In the field you will find a plowman with two oxen. He is to be your Duke.'"

"And," one of the servant girls kneading dough said, "that's when she handed them clothes fit for a Duke to give him to wear."

"Yes," Katianna said, still cleaning between Viktor's toes. "And then she told them to follow her white horse. The white horse led them straight to a man named Premsyl. She told them they would find him eating off of an iron table."

"And they did!" one of the other ladies in the kitchen said. She was basting venison over a fire in the other hearth.

"Yes," Katianna agreed, "and Premsyl is the ancestor of the kind Duke Wenceslas. Now hold still. I have just one more foot to do, you little toad."

Viktor giggled. He had to admit that being clean was a feeling he liked very much, and seeing his mother smile made getting his toes cleaned all worth the while.


"When do we eat?" the lad asked the kind woman. He was beginning to like Katianna, and though she pretended to be harsh and mean, she really liked Viktor, too.

"Here," she said, handing him a crust of bread, "this will tide ye over. Now, let me see the nails on your hands." She reached for her knife and went toward him.

"Nay!" he screamed, and dove under the table. A large hairy boar's head fell off the table and fell right beside him on the floor. The dead boar's eyes stared right at him, and Viktor screamed again and scrambled out from underneath the table and into the apron of Katianna.

"What ye be screamin' for, lad?" Katianna asked. "I ain't gonna hurt ye none. I aim to clean out yer fingernails is all."

He looked at her sideways. His fingernails? Why on earth would anyone care if his fingernails were clean or not? And where was that scary hairy boar that had terrified him and what was it doing in the kitchen?

"Is it dead?" he asked.

"Is what dead?" Katianna asked.

"The boar. Is it dead? I don't want it to eat me the way it ate me father's leg!"

"Shhhh, hush now child," the woman said, gathering him into her arms. "That boar is quite dead. Shhhh. Let me see your fingernails now, and we will finish our story. The Duke likes his boys clean at his feasting table," she said.

"Now, sit still here on me lap and let me have a look at ye. Ye want to hear the rest of the story don't ye?"

The boy nodded. He was shaking, but he did very much want to hear the rest of the story.

Katianna plopped him on her lap and began to tell him more about the Duke's family.

"Now, listen to me closely. Several generations later, in the year 859 AD, another Prince was born into the Premsyl family named Borivaj I. And at the same time in the land of Serbia, the prince Slavibor's wife had a beautiful little daughter named Ludmila. And even though they were 450 miles apart, when Ludmilla was a very young girl, she came to live in the kingdom of Bohemia for she was promised to prince Borivaj. When they were 14 years old they were married in the year 873."

"Soon they were the proud parents of a boy named Vratislav. And Vratislav is the father of Duke Wenceslas."

"At about this time two men named Cyril and Methodius, who spoke our language, came to tell the Duke and Duchess about the King Jesus, the One True God. They made our first alphabet, and that is why it is called Cyrillic – after St. Cryil.[2] They wrote the gospels in our language and the Duke and Duchess learned about the good King Jesus, and began to pray to Him instead of idols and other gods and goddesses. They wanted everyone in the kingdom to pray to King Jesus, too."

"King Jesus? Who is He?"

"He is a good King who loves us all."

"I would like to meet this King!" Viktor said eagerly.

"You will," the woman smiled. "If Duke Wenceslas has anything to do with it!"

"Anyway," Katianna said, carving Viktor's nails into a smooth arc. "The pagans did not like worshipping only this King Jesus. They liked being able to worship many gods and goddesses and being able to do magic and marry more than one wife. They caused much trouble for the Christian Duke and Duchess and for anyone who loved King Jesus.

---

[2] It is interesting to note that many civilizations developed written language after a missionary desired for the people to read God's Word.

"When Vratislav was 14, he married a pagan princess named Drahmoria. Drahmoria refused to pray only to Jesus, and instead preferred to pray to her idols and all the gods and goddesses of the old days. She gave birth to two fine boys – our good Duke Wenceslas and his brother, Boleslav."

"Now, Princess Ludmilla loved her grandsons, and she wanted them to learn about King Jesus. But Drahmoria wanted her sons to pray to the pagan gods and goddesses and them only. This worried the Princess Ludmilla, so she took Wenceslas away from her and raised him in the castle with her. There she had her priest, Paul, help him learn the holy scriptures."

The lad looked at his mother. "The Duke must have missed his mother very much," he said sadly.

"Perhaps," the lady said. "But he loved his grandmother very much, too, and she gave him an excellent education. He learned to read. He practiced his letters by writing in wax, and he even learned Latin, the language of the Romans. He gave his whole life to learning about serving the new God, Jesus Christ. But his brother did not. To this day his brother hates the Duke and will not pray to Jesus." She clicked her tongue and shook her head sadly.

"But why? Why does his brother hate him if he is so good?"

"Just because you are good," she said, "doesn't mean people will like you. They didn't like the King Jesus, either, and even killed Him in the end."

The lad nodded. Even in his young life, He had seen many people die. Children saw many ugly things during the Middle

Ages, so it came as no surprise to him that the King Jesus and the Duke had enemies, too.

"Duke Wenceslas' father died when he was only 13 years old," the woman said. Viktor interrupted her.

"Aye?! As my father has died?! The poor Duke! He lost both his mother and his father, too?"

"Aye, yes," the woman said. "So his grandmother had a very strong influence on him and they had a very close relationship. He loved his grandmother very much, and she taught him everything she could about being kind and serving King Jesus. But alas, his mother was evil, and she hated his grandmother. So she ordered the government to kill Wenceslas' grandmother, the dear Duchess Ludmilla, so she could be on the throne until the Duke was eighteen years of age."

"Nay!" he cried.

"Aye, it were bitter days then. But when Duke Wenceslas became the Duke in charge, he built church buildings for the One True God. He is a brilliant architect and builder. No one has ever seen buildings of such advanced design. The rotunda of St. Vitus, right here at the castle, is the most remarkable building anyone has seen. I will have Tatianna show you later."

The woman just kept working on Viktor's nails. Viktor could not stop staring at the round face as it spoke of such amazing things.

"He also built the church of St. George, and had his grandmother's body moved and buried there.[3] And he wrote the first book ever written in our own language about his

---

[3] Princess Ludmilla is still buried at St. George's Basilica in Prague.

grandmother."

"I have heard of books. I would like to see one," the lad said.

"If you are here long, the Duke will see to it that you see a book or two," she chuckled.

"Aye," one of the youngest girls said.

"Tell him about the miracles that happen at the Duchess Ludmilla's grave," one of the younger girls whispered.

"Aye, 'tis true," an old, wrinkled woman clucked. She was plucking a big black bird whose dark feathers flew to the floor and in her lap. They were even sticking to the wrinkles on her face.

"Well, I have heard," Katianna said, "that people are healed at her grave, and that a sweet scent comes forth from it."

The boy's eyes were large. He looked at his mother and she was sitting as still as he was, with wide eyes, listening to the story. She loved stories, too.

"In yer travels, do ye remember seeing a huge old oak tree beside our border castle?" the woman asked, her arms around his waist.

The boy nodded. "Aye."

"Well, they say that the Duke's grandmother, Ludmilla, planted that tree after he was born, and that the nannies of Duke Wenceslas used his bathwater to water it. That is why it is so tall and still stands there today."[4]

---

[4] The fabled oak tree still stands in the grounds of what was once a border castle, Stochov, where according to legend, Duke Wenceslas was born.

"Ayyyyyye," the boy said. He had often admired that tree and had even hidden up in its branches when running from slave traders.

"As Wenceslas grew up, he also attended a Latin school in Budec. He prayed and worshipped God. He loved God so much that he had even thought of being a priest himself. He considered giving the kingdom of Bohemia to his brother. But his brother is a pagan, and the Duke wants to tell as many people about King Jesus as he can. His grandmother had taught him that a ruler has great influence on the people he rules."

"He has always been a hard worker," one of the littler girls said. "He likes to help in the vineyards and at threshing time so he can help prepare the fruits of the harvest for Holy Communion."

"Yes. And the very priests that the Duke's mother tormented and tortured – the Duke now uses as his advisors," the woman with black feathers on her face said.

"He is a goodly Duke," said Katianna, still working on his nails. "He provides shelter to orphans, buys children from slavery, and is always giving to the poor. Once, when the Duke Radslav wanted to go to war, the Duke instead challenged him to a duel, just to save lives."

"And no matter what time of the day or night, if word is brought to him that any of his subjects is ill or in need, he sends help at once," a little girl said, handing him a small cup of milk.

"Just like he sent help for us," the boy said to his mother. "Aye, what a good man he be."

"Aye," they all said.

"We, all of us here in this room, were once on that slave

block. And the Duke bought us all."

All the women and children nodded. No wonder they all enjoyed their work so much. It was easy to work hard for a master that you loved.


Young Viktor could not believe his eyes. He was escorted by Katianna, into a long hall full of people laughing and singing, where the Duke sat at the middle of a heavy long table so full of food, that Viktor strained to see it all at once. His eyes wandered up and down the table that stretched from one end of the room to the other, and he wondered how there could ever be so much food in one place.

"Welcome, welcome!" the good Duke Wenceslas said, motioning for the lad to sit beside him. "Come, sit with me at my table, young man. You and your mother, come, sit here beside me."

Everyone in the room stopped talking and looked at the young man and his beautiful young mother. It was no secret to anyone that the Duke often rescued orphans and the poor. But to have them sit at a table fit for a king? What kind of nonsense was this? Duke Wenceslas' brother rolled his eyes and the women standing with him looked scornfully at Viktor's mother, Ivana. Thankfully, she did not notice. Her eyes were on the Duke and the roasted boar's head sitting in front of him with an apple in its mouth.

"Come, come. Let us all join in a prayer of thanksgiving to our King for this bounty," the Duke said, motioning for everyone to take their seats.

"*You* are the *Duke*?" Viktor gasped. It was the same man who had bought him from the slave trader!

The Duke laughed merrily. "Yes, my son, it is I! Duke Wenceslas. And I do not eat children and their mothers." He laughed again. "Are ye not hungry? Come here lad, and sit!"

"I'm starving!" Viktor said. "Can we eat now?"

"In good time. First, we must give thanks to the King of Kings for our bounty."

"The King Jesus?" Viktor whispered to the Duke.

"Yes!" he said. "Do you know Him?"

"No, not yet," Viktor said. "But I would like to."

"Very well," the Duke said. "I shall introduce you to Him very soon."

"Let us pray!" the Duke said, and motioned for an old priest sitting near him to begin the prayer of thanks.

Then, food was passed and tossed and eaten with fingers, for in those days, it was the mannerly way to dine. Viktor ate until he felt as if he had swallowed a large bag of stones. He had never been so full in all of his life.

"And now," the Duke said. "Let us, on this St. Stephen's Day, tell the story of the good martyr Stephen, who gave his life as a martyr for Christ. In honor of his bravery, we share our bounty with the poor. It is in his memory I have invited young Viktor, and his mother, Ivana to our table."

Viktor's mother blushed and looked down at her hands, but Viktor beamed and smiled brightly as the Duke began to tell about the Saint Stephen. He told how Stephen died telling others how to give their hearts to Jesus, who died on a Roman cross for all their sins. Viktor admired Stephen's courage but he could hardly wait to learn how to give his heart to Jesus, too, and he wanted to learn more about Him.

"Even now," the Duke said. "There are those right here in the great land of Bohemia, that would like to see the Christians conquered and stoned as Stephen was. But thanks to my dear Grandmother, Ludmilla, one day, all of Bohemia shall be Christian."

Everyone except for the Duke's brother, Boleslav, raised a glass to the Duke. Boleslav did not want a Christian Duke to rule Bohemia, and he and his mother wanted him out of the way.

After much laughter and singing, the Duke walked Viktor to his sleeping quarters. They stopped to look out of a window and admire the moon shining crisp and clear on the sparkling winter snow. It was a bitter cold night, and the Duke was troubled to see a peasant in rags collecting twigs to make a fire.

"Do you know that man, Viktor?"

"Aye, I do," Viktor said. "He has three wee babes and a wife who has been ill. There is no one to care for the lot of them."

"Where does he live?"

"A long way hence, Sire, by the St. Agnes Fountain in a little cave of a house."

The Duke took Viktor by the shoulders and said, "Go back to the hall, gather up as much food as you can, along with plenty of pine logs. We will take these to him and his brood. Go on now."

Viktor did exactly as he was told, and with his mother's help, took all that they could carry back to the Duke. The Duke strapped much of it onto his own back, and helped Viktor attach the rest of it to his.

"Let's go lad. It is St. Stephen's Day!"

Viktor was tired and he didn't want to go back out into the cold, but how could he not do this kind Duke's bidding? The Duke had done ever so much for him. He followed him out into the bitter night.

They hiked for a very long time, and Viktor could no longer feel his toes they were so cold. He felt faint and wanted to stop and sleep.

"Good Sire," he gasped. "I can't go on. It is so dark and cold and I am so weak."

The Duke turned to the lad and touched him on the shoulder.

"Step in my footprints, Viktor, and they will warm ye. We are almost there."

Viktor walked in the footsteps of his Duke. And somehow, he was indeed warmed by them. How could he know, tromping through the snow on that cold wintry night, that nearly a thousand years later, a man named John Neale would write a poem about him[5] and the good Duke Wenceslas. It was set to the music of "Tempus Adest Floridum," a 13th Century spring carol first published in the Swedish *Piae Cantiones* in 1582. From the time of its beginning, Christians around the world would sing this song at Christmastime.

Irony surrounds this hymn we sing each Christmas. First, it was written to the tune of a *spring* song, and it is not

---

[5] Viktor is a fictitious character.

a Christmas carol at all, but a St. Stephen's day song! And secondly, King Wenceslas was not really a king; he was a Duke. But he imitated his King Jesus by caring for the poor, building shelter for widows and orphans, and through helping others in need. Today, a statue of him on his horse stands at Wenceslas Square in Prague. Some people in Czechoslovakia believe that St. Wenceslas will return on a white horse and bring his people everlasting peace.

Paganism and Christianity have been mixing in the Slavic[6] lands for centuries. It is intriguing that the return of Christ and the "return" of the Good King Wenceslas are described so similarly!

## Good King Wenceslas
*Words by John Neale, 1853*
*To the tune of "Tempus Adest Floridum"*

*"Good King Wenceslas looked out on the Feast of Stephen,*
*When the snow lay round about, deep and crisp and even.*
*Brightly shone the moon that night, though the frost was cruel,*
*When a poor man came in sight, gathering winter fuel.*

*"Hither, page, and stand by me, if you know it, telling,*
*Yonder peasant, who is he? Where and what his dwelling?"*
*"Sire, he lives a good league hence, underneath the mountain,*
*Right against the forest fence, by Saint Agnes' fountain."*

---

[6] It is interesting to note that the word "slave" actually comes from this word. Slave trade of Slavic peoples – mostly women and children -- thrived during Wenceslas' time.

*"Bring me food and bring me wine, bring me pine logs hither,*
*You and I will see him dine, when we bear them thither."*
*Page and monarch, forth they went, forth they went together,*
*Through the cold wind's wild lament and the bitter weather.*

*"Sire, the night is darker now, and the wind blows stronger,*
*Fails my heart, I know not how; I can go no longer."*
*"Mark my footsteps, my good page, tread now in them boldly,*
*You shall find the winter's rage freeze your blood less coldly."*

*In his master's steps he trod, where the snow lay dinted;*
*Heat was in the very sod which the saint had printed.*
*Therefore, Christian men, be sure, wealth or rank possessing,*
*You who now will bless the poor shall yourselves find blessing."*

## Epilogue

The life of Wenceslas came to an abrupt and tragic end. When the Duke was just 28 years old, his brother Boleslav tricked him into going to church for prayers and had him murdered in front of the door of the church of Sts. Cosmas and Damian. His statues and the story of his life and death are still displayed there.

*About the author:*

Karla Akins has over twenty-five years of combined experience as a homeschool educator, pastor's wife, author, singer, pianist, composer and speaker. Her two oldest children have graduated from their family's homeschool program and are now married with children. Karla loves being a grandmother! She resides  in North Manchester, Indiana with her husband, Eddie, and their three youngest sons. Her hobbies include Bible study, blogging, and reading. Karla has a tender heart toward animals, and especially enjoys her three dogs: Oskar, a lazy Dachshund; Frankie, a comical Pug; and Gretchen a very friendly, happy Rottweiler.

*I thank the Lord for all His good gifts.*
*I thank my family for their unwavering support:*
*my mother, my sister and my brother, my six children, and my*
*wonderful husband.*

*And I thank my fourth-grade teacher, Mr. Michael Valldes, who*
*first called me a Writer.*

My Grandmother, the Queen

# ELEANOR of AQUITAINE

*by Virginia Swarr Youmans*

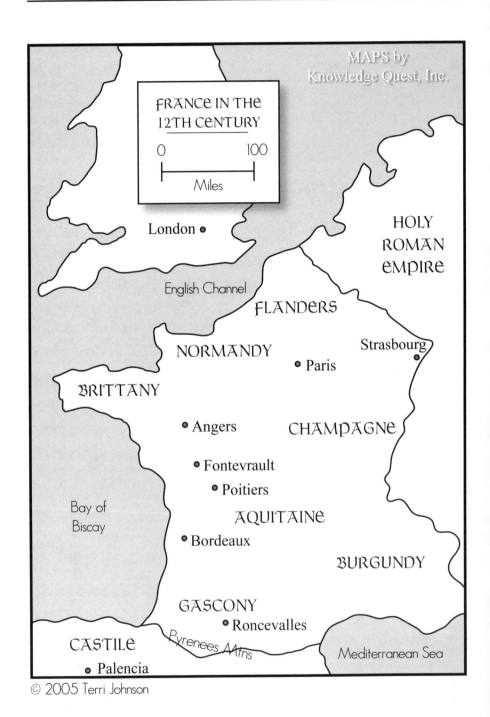

MAPS by
Knowledge Quest, Inc.

FRANCE IN THE
12TH CENTURY

0                    100
|———————————|
Miles

London ●

HOLY
ROMAN
EMPIRE

English Channel

FLANDERS

NORMANDY

Strasbourg ●

● Paris

BRITTANY

● Angers

CHAMPAGNE

● Fontevrault

● Poitiers

Bay of
Biscay

AQUITAINE

● Bordeaux

BURGUNDY

GASCONY

● Roncevalles

CASTILE

Pyrenees Mtns

Mediterranean Sea

● Palencia

© 2005 Terri Johnson

# 5

## My Grandmother the Queen

# ELEANOR OF AQUITAINE

### *by Virginia Swarr Youmans*

This is the journal of Blanche of Castile, granddaughter of Eleanor of Aquitaine (1122-1204), describing what I learned from my grandmother during my brief time with her. (The journal itself is fictional, but the characters and events within it are based on actual events)

*January 6, A.D. 1200*

 am Blanca of Castile, and I received this journal today as a gift for Kings' Day, or what we celebrate as the Feast of the Epiphany, and I have decided to use it to keep a record of my life. Someday I may wish to remember some important event or how I felt on a certain day, and I think a journal is a good way to accomplish this. And so I will try to faithfully write a few lines at least once a week.

I learned today that our grandmother is on her way to visit us. As our dear mother the queen is constantly reminding us all, our grandmother is not like most people's grandmothers, sitting in a quiet corner by the fire, working on her embroidery or singing lullabies to her grandchildren. Ah, no! Our grandmother is Eleanor of Aquitaine, at times the most famous, the most powerful, the most beautiful, the most beloved, and the most reviled woman in Christendom. (I have heard the servants say so many a time.) My mother is named for her, and I can tell by the way her eyes sparkle as she describes her that she loves her mother and is very proud of her.

We children have learned much of the history of the kings and queens of Europe and England, since we are related to most of them and since we are expected to learn from the stories of their lives how to behave or, in some cases, how *not* to behave. As princes and princesses of the Royal Court of Castile, we are tutored in many subjects, even we maidens, for my mother, called Eleanor of England, believes very strongly in the necessity of a good education. My father, Alfonso VIII, King of Castile, does not think it quite so necessary to educate daughters, but my mother gently yet firmly insists that "to educate one's daughters is to educate one's grandsons." This causes my father to ponder and finally relent.

And so my very favorite subject is the history of our family. The family of my father is not quite so interesting to me, since they are mostly Castilian, and we all live here in northern Spain, in the city of Palencia. But the family of my mother is full of intrigues and plots and betrayals and adventures in France and England and the Holy Land, and most of them seem to involve Grandmother Eleanor! And now that she is coming, we will finally meet her for the first time. Mama has written to her at Fontevrault Abbey in Anjou and asked her to come to us, and she is coming! She is seventy-eight years old, and she is traveling across the Pyrenees Mountains through the snow. Mama says she has not seen her dear mother for almost twenty-five years, and I do believe that she is even more excited than we children are! Why she must come right now, in January, and not wait until the spring thaw, I do not know. But she is coming!

*January 20*, A.D. 1200

My grandmother's entourage has been seen, and she should even now be crossing the plains on her way south to us here in Palencia. I am so excited I can think of nothing else! Especially now that I have learned that she is coming to choose one of us maidens to become the wife of the French prince Louis, son of King Philip II. Our mother's younger brother, King John of England, is trying to form a new alliance with King Philip, and Grandmother has been asked to come and make the choice. Everyone says it will probably be my elder sister Urraca, for she is the most beautiful, and she is already fourteen years of age. (Our eldest sister Berengaria is married to King Alfonso IX of Leon and is already a queen!) We had a brother, Sancho, and another sister, Sancha, who were younger than Berengaria but older than Urraca, but they died when they were very small. We also have our brother Ferdinand, who is a year younger than I. And then there is our little sister Mafalda, but she is only nine. Our little infant sister Constanza died last fall, along with our seven-year-old brother Henry. Our poor mother! How sad she must be to have lost so many of her children. But she says that she is blessed to be allowed to keep the ones she has, since so many babies are taken home to the Lord before they reach fullness of years. But Mama is only a little past forty years of age, so, Lord willing, she can still have more children.

I am twelve, and certainly old enough to be married, but I am tall and plain, so I am sure Grandmother Eleanor will choose Urraca. She is so pretty and gay, but very silly sometimes. I wonder what kind of queen she will make, for, if it is the Lord's will, Prince Louis will certainly become King of France someday when his father dies. I pray that Urraca will seriously consider her new role and pray to God to help her fulfill her duties, as our mother has taught us that this is a very serious thing, not to be taken lightly.

I wonder to whom my father and mother will choose to give me in marriage, when the time comes?

*January 25, A.D. 1200*

Our grandmother arrived today, and, oh, what a wonderful lady she is! Mama was right–she is still very beautiful, even in her old age. Everyone says how much I favor her, and I take that as the highest compliment, for she is quite regal. We have been hearing so many stories and legends about her in the past few weeks, and we have even heard the troubadours sing ballads about her that Mama says were composed many, many years ago. Oh, I cannot wait to sit down with her and ask her to tell me the stories that inspired those ballads.

But first we must have feasting and ceremonies and visits by so many dignitaries and vassals of our father. Urraca is quite

bored with it all, although she loves the opportunity to wear fine dresses and talk with young men. But I am fascinated just watching our grandmother during these events–how she carries herself, how she sits, how she concentrates while listening to someone speak. I can see that my mother has learned much of what she knows from studying our grandmother, and I plan to learn from watching the both of them.

*January 26, A.D. 1200*

Today I had some time alone with my grandmother, and I asked her to tell me about the crusade that she and her first husband led to free the Holy Land from the infidels, the story that has inspired the songs that the troubadours sing. (She was married to King Louis VII of France at that time. It is his son Philip who is king now, and his grandson Louis who is to marry one of us.) But instead of smiling and telling me all about it, her face looked sad and her eyes got a distant look in them as she remembered those times so very long ago. "Do not honor me for those times, my dear," she said quietly. "I was but a foolish woman then, not knowing or caring what I was doing or where I was going.

"So many men died on that journey," she continued, "and we accomplished nothing. It was the end of my marriage, because I was too blind to see what I was doing." She sighed and looked as if she were about to cry. But then she told me some more of her story. I will retell it here as best I can.

Grandmother was fifteen in the year of Our Lord 1137 when her father, William X, Duke of Aquitaine, died, making her the heiress of the beautiful lands of Aquitaine, which extended from the Atlantic Ocean on the west nearly to the Rhone in the east, from the Pyrenees in the south to the Loire in the north. She also became Countess of Poitou, and the city of Poitiers was its capital. What a beautiful, fertile country Aquitaine must be, according to Grandmother. The Romans named it Aquitania for the many streams and rivers that run through it.

Her mother had died when she was only a little girl, and she and her younger sister Petronilla grew up rather wild in their father's household, with only servants to watch over them. They were not very demure young ladies, but they did learn all of the things that proper young ladies were supposed to learn–sewing, embroidery, weaving, music, and dancing.

It was the singing and dancing that she loved the best. Her grandfather, Duke William IX, had been a famous troubadour who composed many love songs. Some say that he was the very first troubadour. And his songs were written in the local dialect, so that everyone could sing them and understand them. Grandmother says that some of the songs that we heard last night were actually written by him many years ago. She thought he was a gallant knight, a true courtly gentleman. But she was only five years old when he died, and she realizes now that he had his faults, too.

"They say he tired of his first wife, Ermengarde, and had the marriage annulled," she said, "and sent her off to live in the convent at Fontevrault. His second wife, my grandmother, was Philippa of Toulouse, the widowed Queen of Aragon, and with her he had two sons–my father and my uncle Raymond–and five daughters. But he eventually tired of her, too, and sent her off to the same convent. Then he eloped with a woman named Dangereuse who was married to another man. Eventually he forced my father, William, to marry Dangereuse's daughter, Aenor, and I was born about a year later. So," she said with a wry smile, "I have the dubious distinction of knowing that my paternal grandfather, a married man, carried off my maternal grandmother, a married woman, that they forced their children to marry each other, and that I am the result of all of this family history. And," she said, looking sharply at me and patting my arm, "so are you."

As I pondered that thought, she continued with her story. "We had a little brother, Petronilla and I, whose name was William Aigret, but, alas, he died as a child, from the same sickness that claimed our mother. And so my father taught me all of the things he would have taught his son, preparing me to take on the role of Duchess of Aquitaine when he died. He had no intention of marrying again to produce another male heir, and he decided instead to treat me as his heir. When he toured his lands, he took the whole household along, and I learned much from watching him as he met with his vassals, collected his shares of the harvest from his estates, and held court at the entertainments that were put on each night in his honor. Oh, what wondrous feasts we had! And the music!"

She looked into my face with eyes that had grown suddenly serious.

"Tell me, Blanche," she said, using the French form of my name. "How would you feel about becoming the wife of the future king of France?"

I was very much surprised at this question, for I have

believed all along that Grandmother was going to choose Urraca for this role. "I? Louis's bride? What about Urraca?" I must have appeared to be daft as I stammered and stared at her. But she just smiled.

"Yes, you, dear girl. I have been watching you, and I think you are better suited to this work than is your sister." Putting up her hand at my protests, she said, "Now, do not trouble yourself about Urraca. We will find someone suitable for her, and she will be quite content. But this bridegroom will be king of France one day–my own liege lord!–and so we must be careful to choose a wife for him who will be wise, and patient, and diplomatic, and..."–here she smiled impishly– "someone who will look after the Plantagenet interests with an eye to the future."

I know from my studies that our grandfather King Henry II was from the family called Plantagenet, which got its name from his father Geoffrey, Count of Anjou, who wore a sprig of broom, or *planta genista*, in his cap. But what I did not know much about was how Grandmother stopped being the wife of the King Louis VII of France and became instead the wife of the future King Henry II of England. And my head was spinning with the realization that now I, Blanca of Castile, was possibly going to become the wife of the future King Louis VIII of France!

I turned to Grandmother imploringly. "Dear Grandmother, please continue with your story! I want to hear about your life as Queen of France and Queen of England."

Just then the bell rang for evening prayers, and my grandmother put her finger to my lips. "Wait, my dear child.

We shall have time for storytelling another day. I shall be staying on here in Palencia for a few months. And, Lord willing, you will be traveling north with me to meet your bridegroom. Now let us join the family for vespers. We have much for which we should be thankful."

Such a great deal to think about! As I write this I am only now beginning to realize that God's plan for my life is unfolding before me. I have very little time left to learn as much as I can from my mother and my grandmother about how to be a queen! I pray our Lord will help me to fulfill this calling to His glory. Amen.

*February 7*, A.D. 1200

Throughout this past week I have been unable to write because of my concern for my grandmother. She has taken to her bed, but she assures us that she is only catching up on needed rest and will soon be back to her normal self. Our mother took us all aside and cautioned us to be kind and thoughtful of Grandmother, reminding us of her age and of the losses she has recently suffered. Oh, how thoughtless of me! I was so caught up in the excitement of meeting her and talking with her and planning my own future with her that I had completely forgotten that she is still in mourning for her most beloved son Richard, King of England, the Lion-Heart, who died only last year. While we were burying our own dear little Henry and baby Constanza, Grandmother was burying her Richard, "the staff of her age, the light of her eyes," as she wrote to Mama. And then, just a few months later, her daughter Joanna, my mother's youngest sister, died as well. Poor

Grandmother! I pray that God will visit her with His tender mercy and comfort her.

Our mother also pointed out that of Grandmother's ten children–two daughters with King Louis and eight more children with King Henry–only two now survive: Mama and her younger brother, King John. How can anyone bear the grief of losing so many loved ones in her lifetime? I ponder this as I contemplate my own future as a wife and, I hope, as a mother. Is that all there is to life? Pain and loss? Will I, too, bear children and love them, only to lose them to death? How terribly sad it must be to bury one's own children. Perhaps it would be better to run to the convent, take the veil, and flee this world!

*March 20, A.D. 1200*

Already I have failed in my intention to write in this journal at least once a week. Ah, well, I will just do the best I can to recall what has happened over the past six weeks.

Although I wished to resume my talk with Grandmother about her early life, the opportunity did not present itself for some time. Her announcement to my parents that she had chosen me as the bride for Louis threw our household into a flurry of excitement. Servants ran to and fro, filling orders for cloth and other supplies, ushering in merchants and craftsmen who were eager to provide the goods and services necessary for the upcoming journey and subsequent nuptials. Messengers were dispatched to my uncle, King John, in England, and to the French court in Paris, telling them that I, the maiden daughter of King Alfonso VIII of Castile, am to be given in marriage

to Louis, the son of King Philip II of France, called Philip
Augustus.

I worried at first about Urraca, that she might think
that I had schemed behind her back to trick Grandmother into
choosing me instead of her–as if that were possible!  But Urraca
just laughed when I asked her about it later.

"Oh, silly little sister, do not worry about me," she said.
"Grandmother assures me that she has a prince in mind for me
to marry, as well.  In fact," she whispered conspiratorially into
my ear, "she says discussions have already begun with the king
of Portugal regarding his son Alfonso."

And so my greatest concern about the upcoming
marriage has been swept away.  But I do have other concerns.
I only wish all we maidens did not have to travel so far away
when we marry.  The common people may envy us our castles
and our wealth and our position in society, but the daughter
of a king or a nobleman knows from early childhood that she
will probably be given in marriage to a prince or a count or a
duke from another country, and she may rarely, if ever, visit
her family again.  And if she is not given in marriage to a man,
she will probably "take the veil," become a nun, and enter the
convent, in marriage to Christ, never to return to the world
outside.  Sometimes even if she is married off, she can find
herself divorced, or her marriage annulled, and she is put into
the convent anyway, if she is unable to produce heirs, or if her
husband finds someone he loves better.  (Even Grandmother
Eleanor was put away once, although she did not become a nun,
as Grandfather Henry intended.)

Anna, the maid of my chamber, does not have such a

perilous future before her. She will probably marry a local man, live here all her life, and never worry that her husband will put her away.

Today when I walked with Grandmother in the castle gardens, I asked her once more to resume her story of her early life, beginning with her marriage to Louis VII. She nodded and walked on silently for a few moments before she spoke.

"As I told you before, I was fifteen when my father died. Although he was only the Duke of Aquitaine, he was in truth more powerful than his liege lord, King Louis VI. The king's nickname," she said with a smile, "was Louis the Fat, because they say he had become too fat to ride a horse. Be that as it may, King Louis had the right, as my liege lord and guardian, to choose whom I would marry, and as my father lay dying in Spain, he decided that I should become the wife of Louis's son. My father had known that in this way I would be protected, for there were many who would have liked to carry me away and marry me in order to gain my lands. The king knew he could gain control of Aquitaine, and the income of those lands, if I married his son."

At this point we had reached an iron bench in the sun, and Grandmother sat down, pulling me down beside her. She turned to me and resumed her story.

"The king's first son, Philip, who had been groomed as the next king, was killed in an accident a few years before. His next son, Louis, was in a cathedral school, being trained as a monk, but the king pulled him out of the school and made him the heir to the throne. And that is how I, Eleanor of Aquitaine, who loved music and dancing and colorful clothes and courtly gentlemen, became the wife of Louis VII, who was more of a monk than a prince. I had been trained to rule a large duchy, and he had been trained to read old books." She smiled sadly. "We were doomed from the beginning," she said. "It is a wonder that our marriage lasted as long as it did."

"Was he good to you, Grandmother? Did he love you? Did you learn to love him?" I asked her anxiously, thinking of my own imminent wedding.

"Oh, yes, Louis tried his best to be a good husband to me. But we were both so young, and we had very little guidance. You see, soon after I learned of my father's death, Louis's father sent him marching south to Bordeaux with five hundred knights, to claim me as his bride. He was only sixteen, you know, and very naive about the world, and especially about young ladies. We married in St. Andrew's Church, and right away we were crowned Duke and Duchess of Aquitaine. As we sat beside each other at our wedding feast, I watched him out of the corner of my eye, and I saw that he was timid and awkward in this new role. He was handsome–tall, blond-haired, blue-eyed–but not at all the bold knight or courtly gentleman that I had hoped to marry." She paused, thinking quietly to herself.

"I suppose I reckoned to myself just then that I would mold Louis into the husband that I wanted him to be," she said in a low voice. "And that is the worst thing I could have done," she said, looking up into my face suddenly. "I do not recommend that you try it with your own husband."

I nodded silently, not knowing what to say. She continued.

"I have learned since then, over the sixty-odd years since

126

that wedding day, that when a woman sets out to change a man, she will end up making him less of a man, or driving him away. Or both," she murmured thoughtfully.

"We began our journey for Paris right away, traveling north towards Poitou. At Poitiers we were crowned Count and Countess of Poitou, and the celebration and feasting continued. I could tell that Louis was impressed with me, and a bit in awe, and I suppose I took advantage of that by showing off for our guests and subjects. But in the midst of our feasting and dancing and hunting, a messenger from the French court arrived to announce that King Louis the Fat had died. And so we soon found ourselves entering Paris as King Louis VII and Queen Eleanor of France."

She rose slowly and stiffly, and it was only then that I remembered that she was seventy-eight years old and probably very tired. We walked back towards the castle arm in arm, and she told me confidentially, patting my arm, "On another day, my dear, I will tell you about Paris. You have much to learn about Paris."

I do not like the sound of that! Oh, I pray that the Lord will bless me and keep me as I obey my parents and follow His will.

*March 30, A.D. 1200*

Grandmother has become a regular member of our household, joining us at meals and prayers, hearing us as we recite our lessons, or teaching us old ballads from her youth. The four of us–Urraca, Ferdinand, Mafalda, and I–enjoy her company very much. It is hard to believe that this kind old woman is the subject of legends and rumors. She has a mother's heart. Our mother has told us that Eleanor of Aquitaine's greatest joy was found in her children, and now I see that it is also found in her grandchildren. It gladdens my heart to see her laugh and smile and pull little Mafalda onto her lap.

Today, after the midday meal, she and I sat by the fire, I working on my embroidery, she writing a letter. I hesitated to disturb her, but I yearned to hear more of her story.

"Grandmother," I began tentatively, "will you soon be finished with that letter? I wish to hear your advice for me about Paris."

She smiled and put down her paper and quill. "Of course, my dear Blanche," she said. "This letter can wait. There will always be letters, but I will not always have my dear ones with me." She paused a moment with a faraway look in her eyes, remembering the past that I could not see.

"When Louis took me back to his palace in Paris, I was greatly disappointed in the conditions I found there. Compared to my sunny palace at Bourdeaux, with its open rooms and gardens and fresh air, that place was like a dark prison. Louis's mother, the Dowager Queen Adele, was none too glad to see me, I could tell at once. She disapproved of my southern ways of speech and dress and manner, and I soon learned that I could do nothing to please her. So I did not try.

"I began to take charge and make changes, as I was accustomed to do at home. After all, was I not the Queen of France? I improved the fireplaces to reduce the smoke, and I ordered a thorough cleaning of the whole place. Nothing was safe from my zealous energy. I trained the servants to keep themselves and their workplaces clean, and I improved the music of the chapel by hiring a new choirmaster. Gone were the old ways of King Louis the Fat and Queen Adele, and here were the new ways of King Louis and Queen Eleanor. I held lavish entertainments, inviting all of my troubadours, minstrels, and ladies and gentlemen. And, of course, such entertainments required beautiful new gowns and other adornments, which I began to order at once from the royal dressmakers.

"And I did not stop at the palace household and wardrobe. Oh, no. I entered into a campaign of training my husband, the meek and pious Louis, to be a brave and gallant knight, the ideal man of my dreams. I was successful in driving my mother-in-law out of the palace and into her own country estate, but I also succeeded in driving my husband to bury himself in books and prayers. I realized later–much later–that I was not very diplomatic in the way I began my marriage and my reign as queen. But at the time I cared only for achieving my own ends, in my own fashion.

"Learn from my mistakes, dear Blanche," she said quietly. "If my years of imprisonment have taught me anything, it is that patience is indeed a virtue, a fruit of the spirit. If only I had been more careful, more considerate, more thoughtful. If I had only prayed for Louis, and sought God's will for our marriage… " Her voice drifted off, and her shoulders sagged a little.

"But if things had been different, I might not have married Henry, nor had my eight beautiful babes, nor any of you dear grandchildren! So you see how the Lord has redeemed the years, in spite of my sinful ways."

I smiled at her and hugged her warmly. Then I waited patiently for her to continue.

"Louis often moved from one extreme to the other," she said. "First he was the brooding monk, shut away in his room, having nothing to do with worldly things. Then, when he got word of a wayward vassal or some rebellious subjects, he would respond with harsh retribution. At first I was excited by this display of manly aggression as he led his troops in swift reprisal against the offending castle or town. He even got excommunicated by the Pope over a disagreement with one of his vassals, the Count of Champagne, over the appointment of an archbishop."

Seeing my look of shocked dismay at this news, she waved her hand in dismissal. "Oh, my father and my grandfather had been excommunicated in their day, too, but they did not let it concern them overmuch. In fact, King Philip and all of France are under a papal interdiction this very moment!" Another shocked look must have covered my face. I suddenly realized that I am going to a kingdom that is under condemnation, to marry into a family that has been cut off from the Lord's Table!

"You must understand, my dear girl, that there is much more to churchmen than just religion. A great deal of their activity has to do with politics and power as well. Perhaps we can talk more about that later." She smiled sweetly at my puzzled look.

Grandmother went on to tell me about the early years of her marriage with Louis, including the birth of their daughter Marie in 1145. But it was not the son and heir for whom everyone was eagerly waiting. Although she loved having a baby and being a mother, she knew that she was expected to produce a son.

I must stop here, for I have been called down to morning prayers and to break the fast with my family. I will try to continue Grandmother's story soon.

*April 10,* A.D. 1200

Such a great deal of leave-takings and farewells! All of my gowns and veils, slippers and jewelry have been packed and loaded onto pack horses, and now Grandmother and I are on our way north to France. The most difficult part was leaving my mother, and we both wept, knowing that we may never meet again in this world. After traveling slowly across the plains, where it is already quite warm and green with spring weather, to the Pyrenees, which still are snow-covered, Grandmother and I, and our train of servants and escorts, find ourselves spending the night at a monastery. This is perched at the very head of the pass of Roncesvalles, and it was a most welcome sight indeed!

"You asked about the crusade to the Holy Land," Grandmother began after we had supped on warm soup and crusty bread in the refectory and now sat before the fire in the great hall. "Well, I regret to say that I rashly urged Louis to lead it, although he was also encouraged by Abbot Bernard. Abbot Suger, on the other hand, had serious misgivings about Louis's ability to lead such a venture. And he and Bernard were both very much against any ladies going along. But I cared nothing for what those priests thought. I had decided that a crusade would be a wonderful adventure, and I and all my ladies would be going along, too. I was twenty-four years old, and I thought I knew everything."

Grandmother sighed and leaned back in her chair. She went on to tell about the excitement of entering the city of Constantinople, with its exotic people and sights, and meeting Emperor Manuel and his wife Empress Bertha. But as they left Constantinople and traveled further into Asia to meet up with the German army, they began to see dead German soldiers and to realize that the enemy was indeed real, and that this was not a pleasure trip. One particularly disastrous encounter with the enemy on Mount Cadmos led to the loss of many knights.

"I am afraid that much of the blame for that slaughter has been placed on me," she said sadly. "My vassals had gone on ahead, escorting the ladies, and the Turks attacked while the troops were spread out too thin, climbing a steep pass through the mountains. Louis was never much of a military commander, it is true. But I suppose if I had not insisted upon bringing my ladies and all of that baggage..." Her voice trailed off, and she slowly shook her head.

What was left of the army continued on to Antioch, where Grandmother's uncle, Raymond of Poitiers, was the prince because he had married the princess of Antioch. At this point Grandmother and her husband began to disagree as to the next stage of the journey, and Grandmother sided with her uncle. Raymond was only nine years older than she, and the two of them got along very well together. He was everything that Louis was not–powerful and strong, yet courteous and gallant. She said that some people started to think that she was flirting with her uncle, and Louis himself began to grow quite jealous. He told Grandmother to pack and be ready to leave immediately for Jerusalem. But she responded angrily that she and her vassals were staying with her uncle and helping to carry out his military plans.

"Louis grew more and more angry, and so did I," she said regretfully. "He reminded me that I was his wife and his vassal, and I reminded him that if I ceased to be his wife, I would take my lands with me. I even told him that I wanted a divorce, and that the Pope would support me, because we were too closely related to be married in the eyes of the Church."

At this Grandmother chuckled to herself. "Everyone knew that at the time we married, and it really was not an impediment. But I also knew that 'consanguinity,' as it is called, can be used to obtain a divorce or an annulment if necessary. At that moment I realized that I was very unhappy in my marriage to Louis, and I suppose that argument planted the seed in my mind, causing me to think more and more about the possibility of divorce."

Louis's chaplains, alarmed at the young queen's behavior and fearing what would happen to the crusade if she withdrew her Aquitanian knights, advised Louis to restrain her and carry her off to Jerusalem, which he did the very next morning. Grandmother's vassals were demoralized by this treatment of their lady, and the secrecy and urgency of the matter stirred up even more rumors about Grandmother Eleanor's character and behavior.

"If you learn anything from my experiences, my dear," she said to me, "learn patience, learn humility, and learn to temper your anger. Those ten days in Antioch have caused me trouble all the days of my life."

Eventually the crusade fell apart, and Louis and my grandmother traveled home to France on separate ships. Grandmother's ship was captured by Greeks, and she was briefly taken hostage, and then dangerous storms on the Mediterranean Sea delayed them even further. And Grandmother learned that her beloved uncle had been killed in battle with the Turks, which made her even more bitter towards Louis. On the way to Paris they met with the Pope, who counseled them to reconcile and save their marriage. But it was already quite damaged, and when their second daughter was born in 1150, it ended the marriage altogether.

And now I must put aside this journal and repair to my bedchamber, for the fire has dimmed and the hall grows cold.

*April 15*, A.D. 1200

I write this entry from a beautiful, sunny chamber in my grandmother's ducal palace at Bordeaux. Oh, this is a wonderful place, very much like my native Castile, except it is more green and mild. When we arrived here Grandmother took me out onto her balcony and showed me where King Louis and his five hundred knights had pitched their tents on the green across the river, over sixty years before, when he came to claim her as his bride. She laughed while describing how he had to be rowed across the river in a small boat, since there was no bridge. And now I am traveling north to meet my own bridegroom, the grandson of that Louis of long ago. What will he be like, I wonder? I pray the Lord will bless our marriage and prosper us.

Grandmother says that after a few days of rest we will continue our journey north to Anjou, where she will stop at Fontevrault Abbey. But I will continue on without her, on to Paris and to Louis and to life as a wife, as a queen, and, Lord willing, as a mother of kings and queens, just as Grandmother is. My remaining time with her is so short, and so I must make the very best use of it, to learn more about her and to gain wisdom from her many years of experience.

During our journey Grandmother has told me so much about her life that I despair of ever being able to remember it all and record it accurately in this journal. But I will try to record the account of her first meeting with her second husband, my grandfather, Henry Plantagenet. She first saw him in the company of his father, Geoffrey the Fair, who had appeared before Louis in response to the king's summons regarding the mistreatment of an officer of the king. Louis also wanted young Henry to pledge his loyalty as his vassal, when he would then be recognized by Louis as the Duke of Normandy. Despite the turmoil of that meeting–the violent anger of Geoffrey, the outrage of Abbot Bernard and King Louis–Grandmother noticed the handsome, athletic Henry restlessly pacing the floor, eager to be off. He was nothing like Louis, but embodied the dashing, powerful leader that she now feared Louis would never be. She knew she had met her next husband.

Within months Grandmother had convinced Louis to grant her a divorce. Such an audacious act for a woman–to divorce her husband, and yet not be sent away to a nunnery! It is unheard of! She regained control of her lands, but she had to give up her little daughters to their father, the king. Once again she was free, and once again she was in danger of being kidnapped by any adventurous knight who craved her valuable lands. Back at Poitiers she sent notice to Henry that she was free, and he joined her at once. Only eight short weeks after her divorce was granted, Eleanor, Duchess of Aquitaine and Countess of Poitou, quietly married Henry, Duke of Normandy and Count of Anjou. He was only eighteen, and she was twenty-nine, and they, too, were cousins, just as she and Louis had been. (But, of course, most of the royal marriages of Europe are made between cousins, since we all come from the same roots and intermarry with each other to consolidate power and land.)

Louis would not have allowed them to marry, of course, if he had known about it in advance, for their combined lands and wealth greatly overshadowed his own. Now the regions of Aquitaine, Normandy, and Anjou were combined into one, and France was once more a tiny little kingdom surrounding the city of Paris. How bitterly Louis must have received the news! He soon attacked Henry in Normandy for his treachery, but had to retreat to Paris in a few short weeks. And now I must marry into this family and live in this city, knowing what my grandparents did to my husband's grandfather! May the Lord guide me and protect me.

*April 18, A.D. 1200*

Grandmother and I journeyed on to Fontevrault, where she showed me the tombs of my grandfather, King Henry II of England, and my uncle, his son, King Richard the Lion-

Heart. My aunt Joanna is buried there, too, as are many other family members. I suppose Fontevrault has become our family mausoleum.

My grandmother has regaled me with the tales of the early years of her marriage to Henry Plantagenet, how happy she was living in her native land once more, governing once again as Duchess of Aquitaine, and often governing in Henry's stead in Normandy and Anjou as he took a force to England to try to claim the throne. Henry's grandfather had ruled England as Henry the First. That Henry's daughter Matilda had been married to the Emperor, who left her a widow, and then she had married Geoffrey Plantagenet. Their son managed to secure the throne as Henry the Second in A.D. 1154, giving Henry and Eleanor the titles of King and Queen of England, in addition to the other ones they already had. Grandmother was once more a queen.

She realized early on that she would not need to mold this husband into a proper king, nor would she have been able to. Grandfather Henry was just as determined and ambitious as she was, and he had a terrible temper, too. But Grandmother was content to mother her children, and she had managed to produce not one but five sons, as well as three daughters, in the first thirteen years. Only one–the firstborn, William–died in infancy. She enjoyed riding around England with Henry, presiding at royal courts, improving the laws and introducing music and art to the culture.

I do not wish to write too much about this period of my grandparents' lives, since I find it sad and difficult to think about. But I will say that Grandmother was content with her life and her new husband until Henry developed a close friendship with Thomas Becket, whom he named as his chancellor, for Henry now turned to Becket for advice more often than to Grandmother, and this greatly pained her. Then Henry named Becket as Archbishop of Canterbury, the highest post in the Church in England. But the two of them disagreed fiercely about the power of the king over the Church, and in a careless fit of anger, Henry exclaimed, "Will no one rid me of this troublesome, lowborn priest?" What he did not know was that four of his loyal knights took him seriously, and they traveled from Normandy over to England and murdered Becket in the cathedral, right in front of the altar.

Grandfather Henry began to lose his popularity with the people, and Grandmother sensed that they were growing more and more distant as husband and wife. Then she learned that he had taken a mistress, named Rosamond Clifford, and had begun to travel publicly with her, treating her as if she were queen instead of Eleanor. So Grandmother retreated to Aquitaine, where she busied herself in administering her own lands and providing for the futures of her sons and daughters. Henry had not allowed his sons to take any part in the government, and the young men began to resent their father.

"And I encouraged them in their resentment," Grandmother told me. "Henry had never been a very attentive father to them, and I wanted them to claim their inheritances. I suppose I was afraid that Rosamond Clifford might replace me, and that if she produced sons, they might replace my sons. So I arranged for them to get support from Louis, my first husband, in an attempt to overthrow their father. Our son Henry tried to gain the crown of England, but he failed. Your grandfather managed to capture me before I could flee to Paris, and he put me under house arrest in Salisbury Castle, where I remained for fifteen years, with occasional periods of freedom to visit with my children.

"And it was during this time that Henry's 'Fair Rosamond' died. Of course, I was blamed for that, too. But I had no power to do anything to her, shut away in Salisbury as I was. Henry tried to make me a nun, to set me up here as Abbess of Fontevrault," she said with a smile. "But even the archbishop agreed that it would never work.

"Oh, I made so many mistakes," she cried, turning her face to me. "Although I had learned many things and gained much wisdom about ruling and leading, still I was foolish when it came to dealing with my husband and our sons. Young Henry began to resent his brother Richard, and he was so frustrated by his lack of power. He died of dysentery when he was only twenty-eight," she said quietly, tears streaming down her face. "And then Geoffrey died in a tournament three years later, when he was only twenty-eight as well. That left only Richard, my favorite, and John, Henry's favorite."

Grandmother went on to describe the rivalry that grew between Richard and John, and between both sons and their father. Often the cause of the quarrel was Louis's son Philip, now King of France. He pretended to befriend Richard and support his claim to the English throne because his own goal was to reclaim the lands that he felt rightfully belonged to France. Eventually Henry, sick and weak, was forced to give in to the demands of Richard and Philip, naming Richard as his heir. As he lay dying he was told that even John had turned against him, and this must have caused him great bitterness and sorrow. This occurred in 1189, the year after I was born.

*April 20, A.D. 1200*

    Now I continue on alone to Paris, leaving Grandmother behind in Anjou. I am not actually alone, of course, for I am accompanied by many servants and knights. I have much to think about as I take this last stage of my journey to be married. Although I am only twelve years old, I feel as though I have the wisdom of the ages inside of me. In my veins courses the blood of my mother, Eleanor of England, Queen of Castile, and of her mother, my grandmother, Eleanor of Aquitaine, Queen Mother of England. I even have the blood of the Empress Matilda, my great-grandmother, and the daring Dangereuse, my great-great-grandmother.

    Even my Grandmother Eleanor has had to suffer losses and failures throughout her long life. She has buried most of her children, and both of her marriages ended in faithlessness and disappointment. Parting from her was very difficult, for I have grown to love her, and I am certain that I shall never see her again. I have learned much from her as I have become acquainted with her during these past two months. I have hidden these things deep in my heart, and I will take them with me to my new role as future Queen of France. With God's help I will be a help meet to my husband, faithful and submissive, loving and supportive. I will welcome all of the children God gives me, and I will be a devoted mother to them, loving them all equally. I will strive to serve my people, my family, and my

Lord with all of my heart.  May God have mercy on me.

## Epilogue

Eleanor of Aquitaine lived to the age of 82.  She died in 1204 and was buried at her beloved Fontevrault Abbey in Anjou, France.  Blanche of Castile married Louis of France on May 23, 1200.  They had at least nine children, and eventually they took the throne as King Louis VIII and Queen Blanche in 1223.  Louis died in 1226, and Blanche served as regent for their son King Louis IX, who later became Saint Louis.

*About the author:*

Virginia (Ginny) Swarr Youmans, 42, is a native of Lancaster County, Pennsylvania.  She is the wife of Sergio Youmans and the mother of André, Emilio, Olivia, Cassandra, Magdalena and Lorenzo, who are all taught at home on their family's farm in southern Tennessee.  Ginny is a freelance  editor and author, and she holds a B.S. in secondary education (English) from Millersville University of Pennsylvania, with concentrations in linguistics and ESL.  She is a member of Hopewell Presbyterian Church (ARP).  A genealogy buff, she enjoys using history, literature and her family tree to make education interesting for her children.  Eleanor of Aquitaine was her 25th great-grandmother.

*I dedicate Joan of Arc: The Maid of France to my knight in shining armor, Rickey Allan Crosby. Twenty years ago he rode up to my dorm on his white Colt and rescued me. Thank you, Rick, for slaying the dragons every day for Larisa, Austin, Keeve and myself. You have valiantly lived up to your name, Powerful Ruler.*

# JOAN OF ARC

## The Maid of France

*by Linda Crosby*

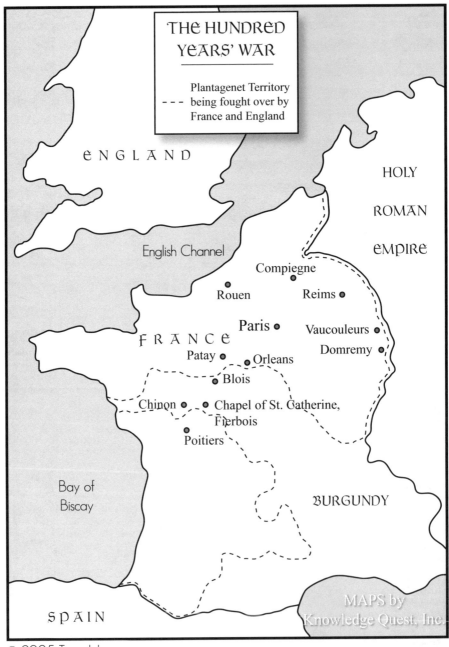

## THE HUNDRED YEARS' WAR

- - - Plantagenet Territory being fought over by France and England

ENGLAND

HOLY

ROMAN

EMPIRE

English Channel

Compiegne

Rouen

Reims

Paris

Vaucouleurs

FRANCE

Domremy

Patay

Orleans

Blois

Chinon

Chapel of St. Catherine, Fierbois

Poitiers

Bay of Biscay

BURGUNDY

SPAIN

MAPS by Knowledge Quest, Inc.

© 2005 Terri Johnson

# 6

# JOAN OF ARC

## The Maid of France

*By Linda Crosby*

France shall be destroyed by the wiles of a woman, and
saved and redeemed by a maiden from Lorraine.

erlin's prophecy, spoken more than 800
years before, ran over and over in her
mind as she rode through the forest in the
moonlight. They were thick in the heart of
Burgundian territory, yet fear found no place
in her thoughts. As her huge horse trotted behind those in the
lead, she was strengthened by the voices of St. Catherine, St.
Margaret and St. Michael.

The three Saints had been God's messengers to Joan
for the past four years. Sometimes she saw a vision of them
in bright light. Other times she only heard their voices. They
first appeared to Joan in her father's garden in Domremy, a

small village on the frontier of the duchy of Lorraine in Eastern France. The Saints were delivering messages that were simple for Joan to follow.

"Attend services at the church regularly," St. Michael had instructed.

"Be a strong Christian girl," uttered St. Margaret.

"Serve others well," encouraged St. Catherine.

However, after they announced God's mission for her life, Joan had pleaded with them for several months. She was a simple country maid only 15 years old with no military knowledge and no horsemanship training. Joan couldn't read or write because, like all peasant girls, she had not gone to school. She was an ordinary girl living in the country with her parents Jacques d'Arc and Ysabelle Romee. She knew her skills well: spinning, cooking and sewing. She loved playing and dancing around the Fairy Tree with her three brothers and her little sister, where they would hang pieces of cloth in the branches. How could she be the maiden Merlin spoke of that would deliver France from the English? It seemed much too grand a mission for Joan, a maid from Domremy, to rescue her country.

The war between England and France, soon to be known as the Hundred Years' War, began in 1337. As the fighting over the thrones continued for decades, England and their allies in Burgundy eventually controlled almost half of the territory in France. The Burgundians were French people living in France who supported England. France's army was suffering defeat after defeat and weakening with each battle. The French city of Orleans fell under siege in 1428. Surrounded by English forts, the people in the city would eventually starve or die of thirst having no access outside the city walls. If Orleans surrendered it would clear a path for the English to attack the last of the French strongholds in the south of France. The situation seemed bleak for the French.

An owl hooted overhead, breaking the silence of the forest. Dressed as a man, Joan sat straight and alert on the back of her shiny black stallion. It was February 26, 1429, their fourth night march; probably five or six more lie ahead for Joan and her escort.

"Praise to God for our safety," Joan proclaimed each day as the sun opened its sleepy eyes and shone down attempting to warm the French countryside. The city of Chinon was in the south of France, more than 300 kilometers away. It was in French territory and Joan was anxious to arrive.

It had been nearly a year since Joan left her small country village of Domremy to speak with the garrison commander Lord Robert de Baudricourt, in the town of Vaucouleurs. Lord Baudricourt had been captain of Vaucouleurs since 1420 and had remained loyal to France. His support was essential to her mission, as she would not be able to travel across France without an escort.

"What do you have to say, Jeanette, that will be of interest to Lord Baudricourt?" Uncle Durand asked again as they traveled away from the family she loved. Though Joan called him 'Uncle' out of respect, Durand Laxart was her 31 year old cousin. Her parents had not agreed to her leaving on such a ridiculous journey but she had persuaded Durand to take her to speak with Lord Baudricourt.

"It is not a message I can speak of until Lord Baudricourt I see," replied Joan for the third time.

She had seen many visions of traveling with knights and leading attacks of war. There had been visions of speaking with Lord Baudricourt and the Dauphin, Charles of Ponthieu, the rightful heir to the throne of France. These visions had strengthened her desire to do as the Saints instructed. Her passion for her beloved France drove her forward. Joan knew that her mission to save France and have the Dauphin crowned sounded foolish to others, so she had told only her family.

It was May 13, 1428 when Joan first met with Lord Baudricourt. She had boldly told him, much to her uncle's surprise, that she needed an escort to Chinon. She needed to tell the Dauphin of her mission to free the city of Orleans from the English siege and have him crowned King of France in the northern city of Reims. Orleans was the key to France's military situation and Reims was the key to the political situation. It didn't surprise Joan when Lord Baudricourt initially laughed at her request. She knew it was an unusual thing to ask, coming from a country girl. However, it was a shock to Joan when he told Durand to take her home and "have this foolishness whipped out of her." Joan was disappointed, but did not give up.

Early the following year, Joan met again with Lord Baudricourt. Although he appeared to be annoyed at having his time wasted with such talk, Lord Baudricourt also knew of Merlin's prophecy. The prophet of old had correctly predicted King Arthur's rise and tutored him throughout his reign centuries ago. Could Merlin have possibly foreseen Joan to be the maid liberating their country from the English?

The first part of the prophecy had recently unfolded with Queen Isabeau signing the Treaty of Troyes in 1420. She was a traitorous French queen, stepping in for her ill husband, Charles VI. With this treaty, she gave her daughter Catherine to the King of England, Henry V, in marriage. This would allow their future son to reign over England and France. Charles, the rightful heir to the throne of France, was declared illegitimate, not the son of Charles VI. This was not the truth, but with the Treaty of Troyes, the French seemed doomed to live under English rule. France was indeed being destroyed by the wiles of a woman.

With the death of his father in 1422, Charles VII became king at the age of 19 when France was in a dangerous position. The English and the Duke of Burgundy had control over most of his kingdom. Charles was in Chinon in the south of France cut off from the city of Reims where French kings were crowned. Because Charles was not crowned he did not have the loyalty of the French people.

Despite Lord Baudricourt continually dismissing Joan, she was gaining support of the people of Vaucouleurs. They too knew of Merlin's prophecy and with France's demise seemingly close at hand they placed their hope in Joan.

It was February 12, 1429 when Lord Baudricourt met with Joan for the third time. Again Baudricourt cast aside Joan's request for an escort. Before leaving however, Joan bravely told him, "Today the gentle Dauphin has had a great hurt near the town of Orleans, and yet greater will he have if you do not soon send me to him." At such nonsense, Baudricourt dismissed Joan. How could she know of a battle halfway across France?

The Saints had given Joan the knowledge of the Battle of Rouvray, a great defeat for France. A convoy of food supplies destined for the English army surrounding Orleans had left Paris accompanied by 1,500 troops. The French defenders were separated into two groups, one having 460 men and the other 4,000 reinforcements. Because of the delay of the larger French troop getting to the route of the convoy, the 460 combatants, who were mostly on foot, charged the English and were soundly defeated. The French lost 400 men that day.

More than a week after Joan had spoken of the battle, the details of the engagement reached Lord Baudricourt and he immediately went to visit Joan. He brought with him his servants and a parish priest.

"How did you know of the battle on the day it occurred?" questioned Lord Baudricourt.

"The voices of the Saints told me of such defeat," Joan answered honestly.

Baudricourt knew that Joan was receiving supernatural help. Because he could not be sure if her help came from God, as she said, or the devil, he had the priest come to verify Joan's story. When Joan received the priest's blessing, Lord Baudricourt prepared her escort of a knight, a squire, and four servants with horses and equipment.

Joan knew that their journey would be through land that was under the control of the Duke of Burgundy, their enemy. Bandits often lurked in dark woods and mountain passes waiting to attack travelers. They might be beaten, robbed or even killed so they could not warn others. It was especially dangerous for a woman to travel on this type of excursion so Joan followed the advice of her Saints and dressed in men's clothing. She would be giving orders to those in her escort, and Joan knew that she would also have more respect if she were dressed as a man.

The people of Vaucouleurs were pleased that Joan was on her way and supplied her with a linen chemise and breeches, a red wool tunic, tan hose, brown leather boots, spurs and a handsome black horse. Donning men's clothes seemed strange to Joan. She discarded her coarse chamlet dress woven from wool and goat's hair and put on the two legs of the woolen hose. She tied these to her linen smock with laces. Next the codpiece came around her slim waist and between her legs to cover the gap between the hose. This felt bulky and awkward to Joan, but with her mission in mind clothing was of little concern. Before her departure, Joan used a knife to cut off her long brown hair completing her new appearance.

Lord Baudricourt himself gave Joan a sword and scabbard to carry. The scabbard was made of hard, thick leather which protected the sword, but was cumbersome when strapped to her side. Joan carried the sword as a symbol of war against England, but she did not intend to use it. She felt that her duty was to inspire the knights and troops leading them into battle, but no blood was to be shed by her hand.


The last night of gingerly crossing hostile territory and avoiding enemy garrisons was followed by five welcomed days traveling in daylight. As snow fell lazily on the countryside and the days were bitterly cold, Joan's mind and heart were focused on meeting her king. There were still rivers to ford that were perilously swollen with the melting snows, yet Joan continually encouraged her companions.

"Our journey will not be in vain," Joan told the men, "for the Dauphin will receive us upon our arrival."

When they were half a day's journey from the Dauphin's residence, Joan dictated a letter to Charles requesting a meeting as well as declaring that she would know him instantly despite having never seen him. As she foretold, he received her two days later.

It was early Sunday evening, March 6th as Joan and her escort were led up the cobblestone streets to the imposing fortified Castle of Chinon high on the hill overlooking the city and the Loire River. They crossed the heavy drawbridge and the manicured castle grounds leading into the grand chamber filled with hundreds of knights, lords and nobility.

The scene before Joan was awe inspiring to a simple maid who had never seen such displays of wealth and grandeur. The large room was brilliantly lit by dozens of torches, candelabras and several fireplaces. Meaty aromas from unknown foods greeted Joan from the far side of the room where a high table was standing on a dais, a step up from the main tiled floor.

The firelight sparkled on the shimmering silks and jewels of the noblewomen and on the armor of the knights. Both noblewomen and men wore tight fitting clothing designed for display, not comfort or practicality. A few ladies displayed extravagant hats resembling steeples or twin horns flowing with meters of sheer veiling. Colorful gowns were trimmed with fur and others with gold wire. Most ladies had their hair hidden beneath gold netting. Several men who were not in armor were garbed in short, brightly colored velvet doublets with padded sleeves and shoulders. They were clean shaven with neatly trimmed hair, unlike those men traveling with Joan.

Lively music, skillfully played by the minstrels on bagpipes, trumpets, shawms, hurdy-gurdies, harps and nakers, came to an abrupt end with Joan's entrance to the chamber. Reports and rumors had been circulating in the castle for weeks about the maid from Lorraine who could hear from God. All those in attendance were fascinated by this peasant girl commonly referred to as a shepherdess in the eyes of the nobility.

Wanting to test Joan's ability to identify himself, Charles removed his royal clothes and dressed as a nobleman in amongst the crowd, leaving the throne empty. Charles was not a handsome man, sporting a large nose and small, sleepy eyes. He did not look like a king. As though none of the dazzling spectacle existed, Joan walked right up to Charles and after making the curtsies and reverences that customarily are made to a king, she humbly said, "God give you life, gentle King."

"I am not the king." Charles lied to further test her. "There is the king," he announced as he pointed to another man in the crowd. To which Joan answered, "In God's name, gentle Prince, it is you and none other."

Charles then asked her name and she answered, "Gentle Dauphin, I am Joan the Maid, and the King of Heaven commands that through me you be anointed and crowned in the city of Reims as a lieutenant of the King of Heaven, who is the King of France. On behalf of the Lord, you are the true heir of France, and a king's son, and He has sent me to you to lead you to Reims, so that you can receive your coronation and consecration if you wish it."

Later, speaking privately Joan told Charles of a secret that God alone could know. This gave Charles great confidence in her and he invited Joan to reside in the castle. Before he would make a decision to send Joan to lead an attack on the English at Orleans, he sent her to the city of Poitiers to be questioned by the theologians and examined by churchmen. At the same time, messengers went throughout the region to investigate the authenticity of this maid from Lorraine. Joan was questioned for three weeks, holding her own against the learned theologians. All reports from those who questioned her and from the messengers came back to Charles stating, "In Joan we find no evil but only good, humility, devotion, honesty, and simplicity."

While waiting for Charles to send her on her mission to lift the siege at Orleans, Joan learned to gallop on a war horse, a far cry from riding her father's plow horses in Domremy. She became an expert at horsemanship and her skill at riding was admired by all those who witnessed her ability. Joan was able to ride horses so ill-tempered that no one would dare to ride them.

Before Joan's arrival from Vaucouleurs, Charles remained locked inside the castle, and had become a pleasure seeking weakling who was ready to abandon the throne and his country. He knew that only a miracle from God could save himself and France from the control of England that his mother had allowed. After receiving the resounding reports about Joan, he decided that she was divinely sent and that he would entrust her with an army to fight the English. Charles was able to raise an army financed by his wife's mother, Yolanda the queen of Sicily. He also supplied Joan with a full-fledged military household, heralds, banners and a full suit of armor.

The suit of *blanc* armor that was designed in the shop of the master armorer for Joan was plain without any ornamentation or coat-of-arms as was common of knight's armor. The sheets of metal that were hammered to fit Joan included a helmet, breastplate, pauldrons to cover her shoulders, vambraces for her elbows, gauntlets for her forearms and hands, as well as cuisses, greaves and sabatons for her legs and feet.

Joan still had the sword given her by Lord Baudricourt, but in a vision she had been shown another sword that was buried behind the altar at the Chapel of Saint Catherine in Fierbois. Joan and her escort had stopped at this church to pray on their journey to Chinon. She sent a message to the priests asking if she may have the sword. No one was aware of this buried saber, but upon digging where she had instructed, a

rusty sword was unearthed with five crosses engraved on it. The priests of the church rubbed the sword and the rust fell off at once without effort. Along with the sword, the Priests gave Joan three scabbards made of crimson velvet, cloth-of-gold and very strong leather.

The pennon Joan was to have in battle was made of white cloth called boccassin and fringed with silk. Lilies, or fleur-de-lys, were sprinkled across the ribbon-like flag and the words "Jhesus Maria" were painted on as well. There was a picture of the Lord seated in the clouds holding the world and kneeling on each side of him were angels. This flag was to be carried in front of Joan by a standard-bearer to show the soldiers where she was. To Joan, this pennon protected her from ever killing anyone in battle.

Charles gave Joan a force of 10,000 soldiers which she joined at the city of Blois along with the convoy of food for Orleans. Joan's brothers, Pierre and Jean, had also come from Domremy to become members of Joan's entourage. At Blois, Joan requested another banner be made bearing the image of the crucified Lord to be carried by the priests. This was used twice daily for prayer to gather Joan, the priests and all soldiers who had gone to confession.

The cry in Orleans planted hope in the hearts of the people, "A maid sent by God is bringing soldiers and food!" Indeed Joan was riding toward Orleans and entered the city by the east gate in the evening of April 29, 1429. Joan and her men were able to enter Orleans with great ease as the English had too few men to completely surround the city. The people in the crowded streets rejoiced and pressed forward to touch Joan and the gallant white horse she rode. As Joan carried her standard, the end of it was set on fire by a handheld torch. Using her spurs, Joan quickly yet gently turned her horse so it could trample out the flame. Those who witnessed this marveled at her skills on horseback.

Upon arriving in Orleans, it was a surprise to Joan that she was not the commander of the army, but one of the captains under Jean, the Count of Dunois. This infuriated her, as she felt like a puppet in Charles' hand. She knew that she was sent by God and the victory would not be won without her leading the army. Joan was the unifying force that brought the downtrodden French soldiers together with the first hope of conquest in many years. She cared for the souls of her army and held strict rules while leading the men. There was to be no swearing and all soldiers must go to confession. There would be no fighting on days of ceremonial feasts. She implored the men to be merciful in their conquest, not burning houses nor stealing from the people. "The army would fight the battle but God would grant the victory!" she decreed.

Joan anticipated attacking the English the following day, but was disheartened by the news that the Commander was unwilling to fight until the reinforcements arrived from the King. Joan believed waiting was useless as her voices had told her the siege would be lifted and their success assured. Still there was nothing she could do without Dunois' command. The delay seemed an eternity to Joan as she went out to survey the English positions four successive days. She had great pity for the English as her voices had told her that the battle was going to weigh heavily against them. In several places the English bastides were within shouting distance and Joan gave warnings to the opposing side to surrender and save their lives. "Go away in God's name!" she hollered, "or surely I will drive you out." Laughter and insults were hurled back at Joan across the demolished sections of the bridge of Orleans.

Finally the reinforcements arrived and the French began overtaking the bastides surrounding Orleans. In the midst of the warfare, Joan told her priest one evening, "Tomorrow I shall have much to do, more than I ever had, and tomorrow blood will flow out of my body." The fighting was fierce with Joan leading the French while grasping her banner and riding her war-horse. She moved swiftly and confidently guiding her soldiers, but near noonday an arrow found its way to Joan and struck just below her shoulder. Joan cried out in frustration at having to be taken from the frontlines. The arrow removed, Joan's wound was tended with an application of olive oil and bacon fat and she returned to combat. The reappearance of Joan's banner invigorated her men who were still coming to blows with the English. When several hundred English saw the Maid's banner, they were terrified and tried to retreat across a bridge. Under the weight of the armored men the bridge collapsed resulting in the knights drowning in the river. Joan wept with pity for all who died.

The final morning of the siege the English formed a battle line to attack. The French lined up with Joan in the center of the troops facing the English. Both sides simply stared at each other for an hour. Surprisingly, the English army then turned and marched off down the river. This was the first English defeat in eight years. The siege was lifted nine days after Joan the Maid had arrived in Orleans. It was a great victory for France and for Joan who rose to the challenges of war. After the battles ended, Joan again wept for those whose lives had been sacrificed on both sides.

Victorious news quickly traveled to Charles in Chinon convincing him that Joan was indeed sent by God to liberate his country. Days later as Joan rode in to meet her king, she did not carry the triumphal air Charles expected. Joan's determination was now aimed at her true mission, to have him crowned the King of France in Reims. Upon meeting Charles she dropped to her knees and embraced the legs of the king pleading with him, "Come as quickly as possible to Reims to receive a worthy crown."

Traveling to Reims would not only be difficult due to English control of that region in France, but the counselors closest to Charles advised him not to go with Joan. She eventually convinced Charles that it was God's will that they move forward with their plans to travel to Reims and the journey began.

En route to the Cathedral in Reims, Joan led many skirmishes against the English. Her greatest victory occurred in an open field at Patay resulting in three French men killed and English casualties numbering over to 2,000.

Numerous letters were dictated and sent by Joan, Charles and those in their company inviting the cities in the kingdom to participate in his coronation. The crowning of a monarch was a celebrated occasion widely attended by royalty and commoner alike. Many from Joan's hometown of Domremy including her mother, father and Uncle Durand made their way to Reims to be present at Charles' crowning.

The ceremony to crown a king of France was deep with traditions, one being that it occurred on Sunday. Having arrived with a great multitude of the French army on a Saturday, the people of Reims hurried to make ceremonial preparations for the following day so they wouldn't be required to feed and house the abundant crowd for an entire week. Another tradition was the use of a drop of oil from a Holy Vial to anoint the new king. The thousand year old flask was retrieved from the abbey of Saint-Remi Cathedral by four knights known as the Guardians of the Holy Vial.

It was 9:00 a.m. on July 17, 1429 when the procession to Reims Cathedral commenced the day-long ceremony of the crowning of Charles VII. Reims Cathedral, also called the Cathedral of Coronations, had been built two centuries before Joan's arrival with Charles. The massive cathedral was the designer's palette for exquisite decoration. The Gothic architecture with bold towers and buttresses was enhanced only by the grandiose stained glass windows that adorn the transepts. As was the case when she first entered the Castle of Chinon, the elaborate surroundings went unnoticed by Joan as she was attending for one purpose alone: the crowning of her king.

First to enter the great cathedral to the voices of hundreds of psalmists singing praises to God were the four Guarding

Knights on horseback carrying the vial. The ceremony included the oath of loyalty by the king, the singing of the *Te Deum*, and the benediction of the royal insignia: the crown, a golden belt and spurs of chivalry, a gold scepter and an ivory scepter called the "hand of justice". With a golden needle the archbishop drew a drop of holy oil from the vial and anointed Charles on his head, chest, shoulders, elbows and wrists. Charles then put on gloves and the ring was placed on his finger symbolizing the union between the king and his people. Wearing full armor and holding her standard Joan knelt proudly beside her newly crowned king and wept with joy. Charles VII then appeared to those in attendance in his royal majesty. In turn, Joan fell before Charles, embracing his legs, and declared, "Gentle King, from this moment the pleasure of God is executed. He wished me to raise the siege of Orleans and bring you to the city of Reims to receive your anointing, which shows that you are the true king and the one to whom the kingdom should belong."

Following the king's coronation, Charles raised Joan's family to the nobility and granted Joan the only request she ever made, to release the town of Domremy from taxation. These acts, however were the last Charles made in Joan's favor.

With six months of fighting behind her, Joan was able and willing to continue the attacks on the English and particularly the Burgundians. Upon leaving Reims, Paris was destined to be the next city liberated by the French Army under Joan's command. Charles, unfortunately, was not so eager to take up arms. He signed a truce with the Duke of Burgundy allowing a three week period to pass without warfare, giving England ample opportunity to send reinforcements to Paris. This battle proved to be more exhausting and difficult than the battle of Orleans. Joan was again wounded, this time by the arrow of a crossbow in her thigh. Her standard-bearer was also struck down and Joan's white banner was thrown to the dusty ground. King Charles sent a message to Joan to abandon the fight for Paris and disband the army.

Another thousand soldiers crossed the English Channel into France during the following six months as Charles neglected Joan's requests to arouse an army and fight. The voices of the saints had originally revealed to Joan that her life as a warrior would last a year and a little more. Unable to sit idle, Joan took matters into her own hands and assembled a band of 400 soldiers who rode to Compiegne where the Duke of Burgundy had laid siege. Joan and her men entered the city under nightfall and prepared to attack an enemy camp on the far side of the drawbridge come morning. Upon first sight of Joan's flowing banner coming toward them, the enemy retreated, however Joan and her men were ambushed and were being dangerously cut off from the town. As they made a final rush for the drawbridge most of her men crossed to safety, but Joan was left standing on the far banks of the moat as the drawbridge slowly rose to meet the city wall. Promptly Joan was encircled by Burgundian soldiers, pulled from her horse by her doublet and forced to the ground a prisoner of Burgundy. The captors tried to force Joan to surrender to them. She fiercely replied, "I have sworn and tendered faith to another than you, and I shall keep my oath."

Joan's life of captivity began that day, March 23, 1430. She was later sold to the English for 10,000 pounds and put on trial by a court and judge that were fraudulent. After five and a half months of questioning and several attempts at escape, Joan agreed to sign a document renouncing her voices on the understanding that she would be transferred from a military prison to a church prison. This was a trick and the transfer never occurred. Joan remained in men's clothing at the military prison and was eventually declared a heretic. The punishment for heresy was burning at the stake in public. Joan's life of nineteen years came to a fiery end in the marketplace at Rouen on May 30, 1431. Joan's last seven words were the repeated name of her blessed savior, Jesus.

Although making no attempt to spare Joan's life during her trial or execution, in 1449 Charles VII called for a new trial for Joan. Seven years later, the original trial was nullified and Charles erected a stone cross in the Old Market at Rouen in Joan's memory. Five hundred years after she died, the Catholic Church canonized Joan of Arc as a Saint.

*About the Author:*

Linda Crosby is a wife and homeschooling mother who enjoys writing in her free time. She has written on Africa and Indians for the Konos unit studies of Stewardship and Attentiveness. History is one of her favorite subjects and she was captivated researching

Joan of Arc for this biography. Linda loves learning with her three elementary age children as they read, scrapbook, fish, play hockey and travel together. The Crosbys are very involved in their church and are known for having a house full of fun and laughter. Linda has a heart for mothers and is leading a mentoring ministry as well as speaking for women's groups. Linda and her husband Rick spent the first ten years of their marriage in Northern Canada but have made their home in Phoenix, Arizona since 1997.

# Pronunciation Guide
### *(In order of appearance in story)*

Domremy – dome-ray-MEE

Orleans – or-lay-AHN

Chinon – shee-NOAN

Robert de Baudricourt – ro-BAIR duh BOH-dree-koor

Vaucouleurs – voh-koo-LER

Dauphin – DOH-fa

Ponthieu – PON-tee-ew

Poitiers – PWAT-ee-ay

Fierbois – fee-air-BWA

Compiegne – com-pee-EN-yuh

*For Nicole and Brady, who have rekindled my love for learning and have sparked in me a fascination for history.*

*Authors note:*

The town of Mainz was located in what is now the country of Germany. Strasburg is situated in modern day France. Then, both towns were simply a part of the Holy Roman Empire. Often these areas were known as the Germanic Kingdom or the Rhineland. Johann (also spelled Johannes) Gutenberg lived during the latter years of the medieval time period. This was a time of great political unrest, marauding invaders and colossal discord amidst the church leadership. Gutenberg's lifetime follows on the heels of the Great Schism and in many ways his personal life was affected by the political and religious upheaval of his times. Many records of Gutenberg's life have been lost through violence and destruction over the last 550 years. Some of the town records of Mainz were burned during the sack that occurred toward the end of his life, others during the reign of Napoleon and still others during the rule of Hitler and the 3rd Reich. Historians have done their best to piece together the details of his life through the court documents that have survived these disastrous episodes during the turbulent history of Germany.

# JOHANN GUTENBERG

## And the First Printed Book

*by Terri Johnson*

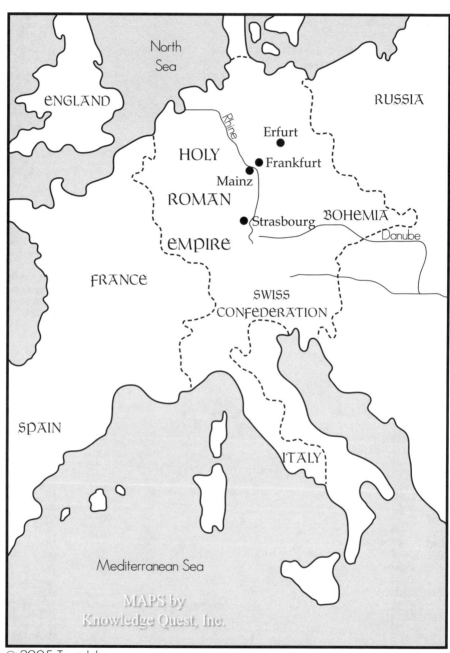

© 2005 Terri Johnson

# 7

# JOHANN GUTENBERG

## And the First Printed Book

*By Terri Johnson*

atching his step instinctively, Johann made his way along the docks which divided the walled town from the great river. This town of Mainz was not a large city even by medieval standards, but it was a busy town nonetheless and a major center for trade along the Rhine River. Johann enjoyed watching the fishermen tossing their catch to the fishmongers and the merchants haggling over the prices for their much needed supplies from the river men.

Johann stepped around the bolts of woolen cloth and stacks of sawn boards with youthful ease and moved past the money changers towards the town square. There was an unusual buzz in the narrow streets as the townspeople talked in raised voices and ran quickly past him. Something strange was afoot, but he could not interpret the cause of the commotion.

Clutching his school book more tightly to his chest, heart pounding within, he ran the rest of the way to the town mint where he hoped he would find his father. As he approached the shop, he noticed that the craft workers were not busy punching coins as they should, but instead were excitedly talking amongst themselves.

"Where's my father?" Johann called with a nervous shout. The men stopped talking and all eyes turned toward the frantic boy.

"Johann," the master craftsman came forward and said sternly, "Get out of here! This is no place for you today. I don't know where your father is, but fortunately for him, he is not here."

The boy quickly turned and raced for home. What was happening today? Where was his father? Although not a coin-maker himself, Johann's father supervised the operations at the mint to assure that the making of the town's money was done properly. This was an important responsibility he carried as a nobleman of the town. Why was he not there today?

As he approached his home on the corner of Christophstrasse and Schustergasse, he saw his mother leaning dangerously out the top floor window of the Gutenberghof, pulling in the wet clothes off the line. "Henne," his mother called to him, "Schnell! Quick! Grab your things! We are leaving town! Schnell! Schnell!"

He joined the other members of his family as they quickly stuffed a few personal belongings into their travel sacks and hurried back down to the docks. The five of them boarded a boat sailing south to Eltville, their country home.

Settling onto the deck of the boat for the 7 ½ mile journey with his sack clasped loosely in his arms, Johann Gutenberg looked back at Mainz, the city of his birth, and wondered when he might return home again. How he would miss the Gutenberghof, his home, and his school chums at St. Viktor!

Eleven-year-old Johann listened as his father told him that earlier that day the craft workers from all the trades had stormed the town hall demanding that they operate their shops themselves. They no longer wanted to be supervised by the lords of Mainz. His father, Friele, had decided that it would be better to leave town while their tempers flared and the violence raged against the town noblemen. Besides, they were terribly outnumbered!

When emotions cooled and normality returned, so would they, his father assured him. His mother Else and his sister, also named Else, were looking forward to their time of retreat in Eltville. It was quieter there. His brother Friele also seemed glad for the adventure and change of scenery. Only Johann, the youngest, longed to remain in Mainz.


The year was 1411 when Johann and his family fled their home to live at their country estate in Eltville. They remained there for 3 years as the turmoil continued to boil between the craft workers and the noblemen of Mainz.

While in Eltville, Johann went to the community school at St. Peters. Here he continued to learn Latin and grammar and basic sums. Every day he would take to class his one and only school book entitled *The Donatus*. It was only a partial

book because he spent a portion of each day copying in his
own hand the text that the school master read aloud. This was
because there was only one book for the entire school. In those
days, all books were hand copied. The students were required
to use their best handwriting as someday another book might be
copied from theirs.

Because books were so rare, they were also very precious
and Johann cherished his school book even though it was
merely a grammar text written in Latin. Someday he hoped
he might own his very own copy of the Bible. His father had
a beautiful heirloom Bible and it was treasured by the entire
family.

In 1414, when the turmoil had died down, Johann's
family cautiously returned to Mainz. Once again, Johann began
to attend the school at St. Viktor, just outside the city walls. At
14, he was one of the oldest pupils at the school. Many of his
chums had already left to attend University or help manage
their family estates. In a couple of years, he would be old
enough to attend University and he looked forward to that day
with his whole heart.

That day finally arrived and Johann left home to attend
the University in Erfurt. He continued his lessons in Latin
and grammar, but he also studied logic, physics, astronomy,
philosophy and debate. Although this university was located
in the heart of the Holy Roman Empire, some of its teachings
went against the teachings of the church. The schoolmasters
encouraged their students to read and interpret the Bible
for themselves instead of relying solely on the sermons of
the church bishops. As a result, Johann Gutenberg would

often spend time in the monastery of St. Peter and watch the Benedictine monks hand-copy the Bible. He would read and absorb the open pages of the word of God, hiding them in his heart. He was fascinated by the beautiful script of the monks, but frustrated by the long and agonizing process. It could take months, sometimes more than a year, for one monk to finish one book. There had to be a better way.

In 1419, Johann's father died and he returned home to take care of his mother. He was now a young man, college educated and eager for whatever lay ahead. By this time both his older brother and his older sister had married. His brother Friele and his new wife had also recently moved into the Gutenberghof. As their family grew, Johann felt less and less comfortable living in his childhood home. It was time to move on and make a life for himself.

Once again, Johann packed his belongings, bade farewell to his family and left the town of his birth. The year was now 1429. Traveling on horseback, Johann rode past rolling vineyards and through dense forests to the town of Strasburg 100 miles to the southwest in what is now modern day France. It was then the fifth largest community in the German Kingdom. The pope himself visited Strasburg around this time and this is how he described the city, "With its many canals, Strasburg has a resemblance to Venice… The town has mansions for gentlemen which are fit for princes."

Johann took up residence at the monastery of St. Argobast a couple of miles outside the walled fortress of

Strasburg. Here he began to experiment in what he secretly called "the art and adventure." He would work long hours into the night, melting down metals, hammering frames and boards into place, thankful for the quiet seclusion of this house at the monastery.

What was he up to? When he hired a goldsmith from town to help him determine the best mix of metals for his project, three gentlemen by the names of Hans Riffe, Andreas Heilmann and Andreas Dritzehn became curious about his mysterious activities. He wasn't quite ready to share with them his most closely guarded secret, but he was willing to take them on as partners on a fund raising adventure he had recently learned about.

Every seven years the church in the nearby town of Aachen held a festival. This church believed that it had three holy relics in its possession – the swaddling clothes of the baby Jesus, the robes of his mother Mary, and the loincloth of the crucified Christ. It was believed that if one could just catch a glimpse of these sacred objects, he would be cured or immune from many diseases.

The priests would hold up the objects from a landing between the cathedral spires during the festival for the crowds below to view. The press of the masses became so great that on many days the city gates had to be closed. The church leaders decided that it was impractical for every person in the Holy Roman Empire to see these sacred objects personally, so they needed to think of a way for the travelers to take the holy and healing rays home to their loved-ones. The solution was mirrors. Mirrors were a new invention of the time and the people were led to believe that if they held the mirrors in the direction of the holy relics, they could catch their healing powers. Once captured and transported safely home, whoever looked upon the mirror that glimpsed the sacred objects would absorb the healing rays.

The goldsmiths of Aachen could not keep up with the demand for mirrors so they agreed that others could produce and sell mirrors for the Aachen festival held every 7 years. This is what Gutenberg and his partners agreed to do and they began to produce mirrors in his workshop. The festival was one year away and they set about making as many mirrors as possible in that amount of time.

They put all of their money toward the project knowing that soon their investment would pay off. They were excited to earn a great deal of money from the sale of their mirrors. Gutenberg was particularly eager for cash to put towards his other secret art – the invention he had not revealed to anyone. Then misfortune struck. Another bout of the plague struck the area and the festival was postponed for a year. Their enormous profits would have to wait for an entire year and they had sunk all of their money into this venture.

Gutenberg had to think fast. Fearing that the partnership might dissolve, he decided to let them in on his most secret invention. But first, they had to agree not to tell a soul and they had to sign a contract stating that if any one of them should die before the invention was completed, his share of the profits would be divided among the remaining partners, with the exception of 100 gulden which would go to his next of kin. Each one agreed and the contracts were written up.

Johann Gutenberg began to tell them about his dream of making books faster and cheaper. He conceived of an idea of making letters, which he called type, that could be arranged and rearranged to make words. The words could be placed together to form lines, even pages of type that could be printed on paper or vellum. These arranged pages could be proofed and printed multiple times to achieve many copies exactly alike. He explained to them that he didn't have all of the details worked out, but that he had lots of ideas he was working on and that he welcomed their time and resources on completing his invention.

Wow! The partners were exhilarated! They immediately threw their energies into this new project. Gutenberg taught them everything that he knew so far about melting down metals, making forms, mixing dyes. They set up a working press at Dritzehn's house in town, while the metal letters were cast at Gutenberg's home at St. Argobast. He did not want to set up the entire printing operation in one place for fear of casual onlookers catching on to his idea.

Once again misfortune struck. On Christmas Eve, Andreas Dritzehn became ill from the plague and died during the night. Gutenberg grieved for his friend. He also worried about the printing press. He sent his servant to Dritzehn's home to take apart the press so that no one could tell what they were using it for. Shortly after his death, Andreas's brother George came across the contract written up by Gutenberg and his partners and noticed something strange. Andreas Dritzehn had forgotten to sign the contract!

George Dritzehn immediately demanded that he take his brother's place in the partnership or he would take Gutenberg to court. Gutenberg refused, went to trial and triumphantly won the case. Unfortunately this legal fiasco lasted nearly a year and the remaining partners grew impatient and lost interest in the invention of movable type. The partnership dissolved and the other two men went off to sell mirrors at the Aachen festival. Meanwhile, Gutenberg began to develop the most crucial part of his invention.

It was called the hand-mould and this small hand-held apparatus became the crux of his amazing invention. Recalling his childhood when he would watch the punch cutters at the mint, he had already decided he needed punches engraved with the shapes of letters. These had to be carved out of hard steel to maintain sharp details when punched or pressed onto a surface. But the trouble was getting those punches small enough and lined up to make easily readable words. A typical page needed some 3500 characters and that was a lot of engraving to do! What he needed was a way to make multiple pieces of type from one set of punches. The hand-mould solved his dilemma.

Gutenberg found that a letter, such as "t" could be carved out of the end of a bar of steel. That "t" would then be placed on a softer metal, such as copper or brass, and "punched" or struck with a hammer to make an impression. This impression, called a matrix, would next be placed into the bottom of an adjustable hand-mould. If the letter was narrow, like "i" or "l", then the sides of the mould would be brought closer together. If the letter was wide, like an "m" or a "w", the sides would be pushed further apart. Finally, a mixture of melted lead, tin

The process from punch to type

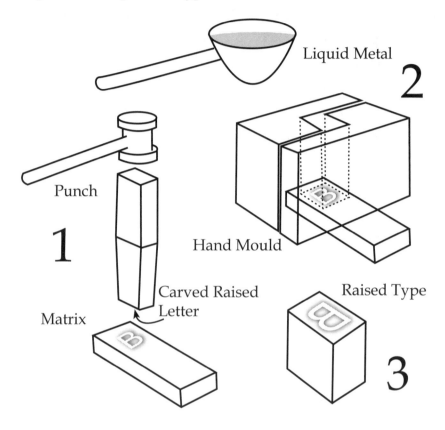

and antimony would be poured into the mould. It would cool immediately, be released from the mould and a piece of type was cast. Many pieces of type would be made from this same impression, or matrix, because a printer would need 131 "t's" just to typeset these two pages alone.

The other all important aspect to Gutenberg's invention of printing was the press. These small newly created pieces of type needed to be arranged into a form and pressed onto a page. After many trials and errors, he had succeeded in constructing a printing press that would evenly press the letters onto a page.

His ink mixture was finally the right consistency and he was ready at last to print a real page from a book for a test run. He chose a page from a popular work entitled, *The Last Judgment*.

After hours of work in setting up the page and years of sweat and hard work bringing him to this point in time, Johann Gutenberg printed his first page. It worked! It could use some improvements, but it worked!

Johann was energized to get underway on printing something, anything, when he heard a commotion outside. Gutenberg had been so consumed with his invention of printing that he had been unaware of the political unrest in Strasburg. The city officials were calling all men into service to protect Strasburg from an attack by a marauding band of soldiers roaming the countryside.

Johann may have felt vulnerable in that he lived outside the city gates or he may have not felt strongly enough for a city that he did not consider home. In any case, he once again packed up – this time with as much type and equipment as he could possibly carry – and he moved back to the golden city of Mainz on the Rhine.

It didn't take him long to get back to work and set up shop. While doing so, a banker named John Fust became intrigued by all of the curious activities at the Gutenberghof. Gutenberg let him in on his secret and Fust became so enthused that he offered to loan him 800 gulden to set up a large printing shop at the Humbreckhof just down the street. Excited by the prospect of a larger shop, more equipment and a staff to train in

the fine art of printing, Johann jumped at the offer and agreed to pay him back in full with interest. He even agreed to give him all of the printing equipment if he should fail to repay the loan.

Six printing presses were built and installed at the Humbreckhof, a staff of 20 plus workers were hired and trained, and a new, smaller typeface was designed and engraved. The brand new printing works at the Humbreckhof was now ready for its first major job. Gutenberg and Fust decided that they should start by printing the best selling book of all time – the Bible.

Before long, work was under way. The beautiful new Bible was set up in two columns and 42 lines. Each page required about 2800 pieces of type. The Bible upon completion would have nearly 1200 pages and its first edition would consist of 200 printed copies. They knew they would have many long months of hard work ahead of them. The task was enormous, but under the direction and vision of Johann Gutenberg, the Bible began to take shape and the printers were becoming experts in their new art.

Johann took on a special apprentice by the name of Peter Schöffer. To Schöffer, Gutenberg imparted not only his expertise skill in developing fine print, but also his standards for perfection. He passed on to him his vision for the printed book to not only be cheaper and faster than its hand-copied counterpart but for print to become even more eye-catching than script. Hand scripted books in that day had beautiful large lettering at the beginning of each paragraph called illumination, each one in itself a work of art. Manuscripts were also of more than one color – often three. Gorgeous borders and pictures were frequently drawn down the sides. Gutenberg wanted his Bible to match or surpass in loveliness the handwritten works of art that currently resided on medieval book shelves.

Schöffer soon became a master printer. Together, he and Gutenberg created what most people consider the finest book ever printed. Today it is known as the 42-line Gutenberg Bible. When the work was nearly completed, John Fust became impatient with the entire process and demanded that Gutenberg immediately repay his loan in full. Gutenberg was unable to do so because all of his money was tied up in the printing of the Bible. He asked Fust for a few months time to bind the books and get them ready for sale. But Fust refused and hauled him into court.

Historians wonder if John Fust was simply impatient, or if perhaps he was truly mean spirited and money hungry. For he did indeed win the law suit and Gutenberg had to turn over all of the equipment and unfinished Bibles to Fust. Fust promoted Schöffer to master of the Humbreck Printing Works and they completed the Bible without Gutenberg. Every copy was sold and with the proceeds they were able to begin setting up for the next printed book – a church hymnal.

Gutenberg was devastated. His life work was practically stolen from him by his trusted financial partner. He was in his mid-fifties by this time and he nearly did not have the heart to start over again. But Johann Gutenberg was not a man to give up easily.

Johann once again set up shop at the Gutenberghof and

in those tiny quarters with his single printing press, he began to print books once again. In his later years he produced many documents and books, even collaborated on another edition of the Bible.

Just when his life was becoming rather routine and predictable, an alarming event occurred. Enemy troops stormed the city of Mainz, overthrew the government and exiled many of the inhabitants. The city folks were corralled in the town square and herded out through the city gates with only what they could carry on their backs.

Dazed and overwhelmed, Johann Gutenberg headed for the country estate in Eltville. Relatives were living in the house, but they cheerfully provided him with a room. Under his guidance and direction, a print shop was opened in Eltville. In fact, printing houses were springing up all over Europe, like a ripple in a pond, as the original printers whom Gutenberg trained were exiled from Mainz and spreading out across the countryside. A printing revolution had been born. Within 40 years, there would be over 500 print shops in operation in Europe and more than one million books printed. Gutenberg had indeed changed the world of book making. He has been credited with one of the most revolutionary inventions of all time.

And so what happened to Johann Gutenberg? After his exile from his hometown, the archbishop heard of his plight and wanted to restore him to favor for his remarkable invention. He bestowed on him the honor of knighthood and provided him with a home in Mainz not far from the Gutenberghof after the city had been restored to peace. Gutenberg traveled back and forth between Eltville and Mainz overseeing the printing works which operated in those cities, but he never again ran the shops himself. He was getting older in years and needed to slow down. One day, while at his house in Mainz, Gutenberg walked past the newly reopened print shop at Humbreckhof and spoke with Peter Schöffer. He learned from him that John Fust had died of the plague during his travels in Italy. Gutenberg grieved over this news because he knew that if it weren't for Fust the Gutenberg Bible never would have come into being. He continued to walk and found himself at the docks. Large ships and towering cranes dominated the landscape. So much had changed since he was a boy. He saw a book seller loading a crate of printed books onto the dock for shipment to Frankfurt. As he passed by, several people nodded to Gutenberg and tipped their hats to him. He was now an honored citizen and a knighted lord. For a brief moment, time seemed to stand still. The bright autumn sunshine glinted off the Rhine River and a sense of peace and accomplishment washed over him. He thanked the Lord for his long and full life as he turned for home.

## Epilogue

Johann Gutenberg died at the age of 68. A clerk at the town hall recorded these words in the city records book, "In the year of our Lord 1468 on St. Blasius' Day died the honored master [Johann Gutenberg] on whom God have mercy." As he was honored then, so we honor him today – for this man changed the world as we know it today. His determination to print the first book has given mankind the gift of easily sharing knowledge and information with one another. Printed books have brought delight to their readers every day for over 500 years. His gift will not quickly be forgotten.

*About the Author:*

Terri Johnson is the creator of Knowledge Quest maps and timelines (www.knowle dgequestmaps.com). Her mission for the company is to help make the teaching and learning of history and geography enjoyable  for both teacher and students. She has created and published over 15 map and timeline products. Her *Blackline Maps of World History* have been widely recommended in the education community and published in *The Story of the World* history series by Susan Wise Bauer. Terri and Knowledge Quest recently won the "Excellence in Education" award granted by The Old Schoolhouse magazine for best geography company of 2003 and 2004. Terri resides in Gresham, Oregon with her husband Todd and their four children whom she teaches at home. She is expecting baby number five any day now...

*For my father, Edward A. Leutwiler, whose passion for truth and love of the written word inspire the generations that follow him.*

# MARTIN LUTHER

## Leader of the Reformation

*by Kathleen L. Jacobs*

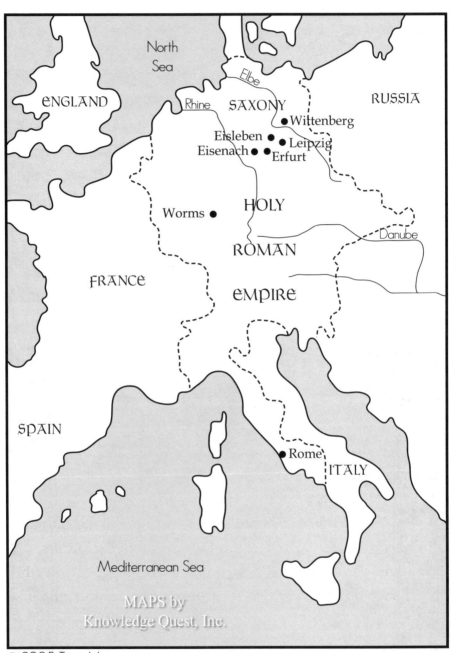

# 8

# MARTIN LUTHER
## Leader of the Reformation

*By Kathleen L. Jacobs*

n April 18, 1521 the most powerful leaders of the Holy Roman Empire gathered in Worms, Germany to defend Europe against a single man: Martin Luther. This dangerous opponent wore the seemingly gentle robes of a monk, yet his words were a sword raised against the traditional religion of Europe. Despite his position as a priest in the Church, he had dared to declare that the Catholic Church's doctrine was wrong because it did not match the Bible's teaching. In reply, Pope Leo X declared Luther a heretic, an enemy of both the church and the truth. The Pope's instructions were clear – Martin Luther must not be allowed to continue teaching. Already, the monk's words had wounded the Church's power and influence throughout Europe. The heretic must be silenced!

Martin Luther came willingly to meet his accusers; despite the fear that certainly battled within his heart against courage. As he advanced through Worms, dodging the thick crowds that had gathered to watch him pass, Luther knew that even his friends believed his death was certain. For centuries, heretics had been swiftly punished by fiery death at the stake. One hope for life remained– Luther could admit that he had been wrong and that the Catholic Church taught indisputable truth.

Would Martin Luther bow to the Catholic Church's demands? Commanded by this question, each prince and nobleman turned his gaze towards the door when the guards announced Luther's arrival. As the monk stepped towards the throne of Emperor Charles V to give his final answer, the gray dusk of late afternoon deepened the solemn hush that had settled over the finely dressed assembly. Perhaps it was fitting that the evening torches had been lit before Martin Luther's entrance; after all, his ideas had ignited passion throughout Europe.

Luther stopped near a table that held a stack of his writings. Many in the room hoped these dangerous books would soon be flung into the fire. An official in a long robe stepped forward and faced the monk. "Will you retract the words written in these books?" he demanded.

Martin had asked himself this question many times – a question well-known to anyone who dares present new ideas. Was he wrong? Were the princes, knights, professors, and Catholic Church leaders who had traveled far to oppose him right?

Martin Luther no longer wondered what answer to give. "I cannot and I will not retract anything...here I stand. May

God help me, Amen," [1] he declared.

Even his enemies watched his courage with amazement while an awed fear must have settled over those listeners who shared Luther's beliefs. Before the most powerful men of the empire, Luther had chosen the deadly answer.

*****

When Martin Luther was born in Eisleben, Germany on November 10, 1483, Europe was a continent in the midst of discovery. By the morning of Martin's birth, Johannes Gutenberg's recent invention, the printing press, had drastically increased the amount of information Europeans had available. In the years that followed, this single invention would allow one man's ideas to rapidly spread throughout the continent. In less than ten years, Christopher Columbus would sail to America. His discovery would force Europeans to expand their ideas about the world. These ideas and the culture of Renaissance Europe would impact Martin Luther. One day this little baby would announce his own discovery – one that would lead him to challenge the powerful Catholic Church.

Martin Luther's humble birth in a poor mining community did not, however, begin to whisper the remarkable future in store for this baby. Martin Luther's parents, Hans and Margaretta Luther, lived simply. His father was a miner, and the family never had enough money. Despite these challenges, Martin's father dreamed that his son would one day practice law. While most children in his village worked to help support their families, young Martin went to school.

---

[1] Quoted in Stephen J. Nichols, *Martin Luther: A Guided Tour of His Life and Thought* (Phillipsburg, NJ: P&R Publishing, 2002), 42.

By age fourteen, Martin had left home to study briefly in Magdeberg and then in Eisenach. From that time forward, he rarely saw his family. These years were difficult. His teachers were strict, and his family could not afford to send him money for food. Martin often joined a group of hungry schoolboys who begged in the streets.

His life changed the day a wealthy family took notice of him. They offered him food and later invited him to come to live with them. Finally, Martin had comfortable shelter, good food, and pleasant friendship. He enjoyed studying and did well in school. His love for music grew, and he learned to play the lute.

These new surroundings, however, could not change the dark thoughts that had already besieged him. He believed God was strict and harsh. He worried that he could never do enough good to please God. As a result, Martin hated God. Even at a young age, these thoughts apparently caused deep sadness and frustration for the boy.

In 1501 Martin eagerly entered the University of Erfurt. By 1505 he had earned both a Bachelor of Arts and a Master's degree. He arranged to stay in Erfurt so he could study law. He was steadily moving towards the career his father had planned for him.

Then lightning struck! Real lightning! In the summer of 1505, Martin visited his family. As he traveled the road back to Erfurt, the cloudy skies stirred into a violent storm. Howling wind and darting rain swirled around him. Thunder shouted deep-throated threats. Suddenly, a bolt of lightning threw the traveler to the ground. Martin screamed a promise to God – if he survived, he would become a monk!

A few weeks later, he invited his friends to a party. Everyone had fun until Martin announced that he was saying good-bye. He planned to enter a monastery and would not see them again. His friends were shocked. When his father heard the news later, he was furious. Hans Luther had planned such a different career for his son!

The night of the party, Martin Luther left his apartment and his university education behind. At twenty-one years of age, he entered a nearby monastery and heard the gates close behind him. Monks lived alone, separate from everyone else. Luther must have believed he was leaving the outside world forever. How wrong he was if he thought the rest of his life would be quiet and lonely!

Luther did not choose the life of a monk just because of a thunderstorm promise. He desperately wanted to please God and zealously pursued forgiveness for his sins. He confessed his sins to priests for hours at a time. Nobody else did that! The priests grew tired of listening to him! These endless confessions were driven by Luther's understanding that if he failed to confess even one sin, God would condemn him. Fear tortured the monk.

Luther hoped his life as a monk would make him acceptable to God. Men who became monks vowed to give up everything they owned and to lead difficult lives. They wore scratchy, simple robes. They ate small and plain meals. They slept in narrow cells. Luther eagerly did all of this and more. He begged for bread in the streets. He fasted. He swept floors.

He slept without blankets in freezing rooms. Luther later said that if it had been possible to reach heaven through "monkery," he would have succeeded. By punishing his body in this life, he hoped to reach heaven after death. He trembled at the thought that he might instead spend eternity in hell or time in purgatory after death.

What was the result of Luther's grand effort to please God? His body became so weak that he almost died, and he became convinced that it was impossible to please God. He gradually concluded that he did not just have a list of individual sins that needed to be forgiven; he was sinful at his core. Martin Luther needed complete and total forgiveness for his very soul!

Luther refused to stop searching for salvation. He began reading a Bible chained to the wall of the monastery. What a rare treasure! Few Bibles existed in Luther's day. Almost no one read the Bible! In church he had heard only small sections read. Now, in the monastery, he read and studied the entire book. Luther knew he would find truth in the Bible. He did not expect that what he learned would ultimately drive him away from the Catholic Church!

Luther continued to try to be as good as possible. In May of 1507, he was chosen to become a priest. Luther later reported that he trembled in terror when he said his first mass. He was so sinful! How could he dare speak to God? His fear of God intensified. So did his desire to be rid of sin.

At this point, Luther came to the attention of two men who would have an important influence on him. The first man, Johann von Staupitz, held a leadership position among the monks and taught Bible as a university professor. The second,

Prince Frederick the Wise of Saxony, was one of the most powerful rulers in the Holy Roman Empire. With Staupitz's help, Frederick founded the University of Wittenberg in 1502. This ruler wanted his university to be one of the finest in Germany, and he needed good professors.

Staupitz noticed Luther on a visit to the Erfurt monastery. He began to guide and encourage the distressed monk. Staupitz decided that if Luther were allowed to study and teach, he might be too busy to think his dark thoughts. Under his direction, Luther moved to the Wittenberg monastery and began to teach philosophy and the arts as a university professor.

Staupitz also encouraged Luther to stop reading the words of men. Instead, Luther must learn theology from the Bible, God's Word, alone. Staupitz made this easier by giving his friend a Bible of his own. He also convinced Luther to take Bible classes, and eventually Luther earned a doctorate degree in theology.

In 1510, Luther took a trip to Rome. He saw monks, priests, and the Pope himself living in luxury. Their clothes were elegant, their plates full, and their buildings fancy. Luther watched in horror. He knew this did not please God. How different from the simple lives of German monks!

Luther returned to Wittenberg. In 1512 he became a professor of theology. This profession allowed him to spend his days studying the Bible and teaching what he learned. He worked eagerly. Luther firmly believed every word in the Bible. The more he studied, the more he realized that the Bible disagreed with what the Catholic Church taught.

While studying during the years between 1513 and 1518, Luther finally discovered how to please God. Imagine how excited he must have been! Luther had always thought that God accepts good people. Sadly, as hard as the monk tried, he could never be good enough! He knew sin affected his secret thoughts and his feelings, not just his actions. Imagine his surprise when he read in the Bible that God knows humans can never make themselves good enough. Instead, God makes people righteous. He read in Romans 1:17 that "The righteous shall live by faith." The Bible had a message of hope for Luther – God bestows righteousness on people who repent and have faith in his son, Jesus Christ. By placing his faith in Jesus, his death for him on the cross and God's amazing forgiveness, Luther at last found freedom from the misery of sin! He knew that after this earthly life, he would enter heaven because of God's grace alone, not because of any goodness on his part.

Not being one to do anything half-heartedly, Luther eagerly desired to share the news of salvation with everyone he knew! He had many opportunities to teach about salvation. Not only was he a professor, he also pastored a church in Wittenberg. Soon crowds gathered to hear him preach. Luther proclaimed a message intriguingly different from what the typical priest taught.

During 1516, Luther's sermons began to criticize the Catholic Church's method of releasing people from the dreaded punishment of purgatory. The Church claimed that the pope could grant an indulgence to a person who performed a specific good work such as praying, giving to the poor, or visiting a particular church.

Sinners could also gain an indulgence by viewing relics – items that were connected to the lives of Jesus, Mary, Peter, and other saints. Prince Frederick had worked diligently to amass an impressive collection of relics at the Castle Church in Wittenberg. The church claimed to house a thorn plucked from the crown of Christ, a piece of gold from the wise men, a twig from Moses' burning bush, and a tooth from a famous saint. Each year on November 1, All Saints' Day, the church offered an indulgence to repentant sinners who viewed the relics and made the required donation. All visitors departed with a piece of paper proclaiming that their punishment in purgatory had been decreased; their coins remained at the church. Prince Frederick used a portion of this money to build a bridge and fund his university!

All Saints' Day indulgences concerned Luther, but his anger increased when a monk named John Tetzel made declarations that endangered the souls of the citizens of Wittenberg. Tetzel traveled from town to town selling indulgences. After a grand entrance through the gates of a city, he began to preach. He made buying indulgences easy. A scared sinner could drop coins in Tetzel's church box and immediately receive assurance of complete forgiveness. Tetzel even encouraged people to buy indulgences for their dead relatives, claiming that souls could be instantly released from the agony of purgatory. After listening to his dramatic descriptions of painful punishment, people paid eagerly.

Frederick refused to allow Tetzel near Wittenberg because he wanted people to buy all their indulgences at the

Castle Church. However, many Wittenberg citizens traveled to other places to purchase from Tetzel. They then told their pastor, Martin Luther, that they could keep sinning without fear of punishment because Tetzel's indulgence covered even future sins!

Luther knew that the people he pastored needed protection from false teaching. Most of them could not read the Bible on their own and believed whatever the Church leaders taught. By October 31, 1517, Luther was angry enough to take action.

Crowds filled the city of Wittenberg on this eve of All Saints Day. As Luther walked down the street, he passed groups of pilgrims who believed that paying money would help them get to heaven. Luther's study of the Bible had convinced him that this practice was wrong. If these people did not have faith in God's gift of salvation, they would enter hell after death. The time had come to declare the truth!

Luther marched to the church clutching a document titled *Ninety-Five Theses*. On the door, he posted this list of ninety-five arguments against indulgences and related matters. An invitation appeared above the list – Luther wished for others to join him for a public discussion of this matter.

Luther's *Ninety-Five Theses* were written in Latin, a language few people in Germany could read. Even so, people throughout Wittenberg soon were talking about Luther's ideas. The *Ninety-Five Theses* were translated into German, and with the help of the printing press, the debate he initiated rapidly spread far beyond the stone walls of Wittenberg.

Luther likely did not realize that he was doing anything

radical by posting his *Ninety-Five Theses* because professors often began debates this way in 1517. He probably did not expect his document to become famous. He merely hoped that pointing out evil teaching would purify the Church. At this point, he had no plan to leave the Catholic Church. In fact, he apparently believed that Pope Leo X would agree with his attack on Tetzel. However, Rome was using a share of the money that Tetzel raised to finance the construction of St. Peter's Basilica, and the Pope refused to speak against these indulgences.

The debate Luther began on October 31, 1517 expanded over the years to include many issues concerning salvation and the Bible's message. While many who read Luther's words responded with defensive anger, others found that his arguments mirrored their own misgivings concerning the traditional teachings of the Catholic Church. The end result was a complete division between the Catholic Church and the reformers. This separation created the Protestant churches of today. The Lutheran denomination even takes its name from Martin Luther. October 31 is now celebrated as Reformation Day because of general agreement that Luther's action on that date marked the beginning of the Protestant Reformation.

Such a radical outcome would have been difficult to predict in 1517, but the Catholic Church leaders quickly realized they had reason for concern. In August of 1518, Luther received an order to come to Rome. He would be asked to recant his teachings. If he refused, he would be arrested. The monk had sixty days to obey.

Luther did not want to go to Rome. He knew that he would probably be killed if he entered the city. The Church leaders had punished another reformer named John Hus in 1415. He had died after being tied to a stake and burned. Luther knew he must be careful in his actions. His words, however, remained daring as he proclaimed in writing that the Pope could be wrong.

The monk turned to Frederick the Wise for help. Frederick arranged for Luther to be tried in Germany instead of Rome. The first step was a private meeting in 1518 at Augsburg between Luther and Cardinal Cajetan, the Pope's representative.

At Augsburg, Luther begged his accuser to show him which of his teachings were false. He promised to admit error if someone would use the Bible to prove him wrong. Cajetan avoided debate. He had one primary question: Would Luther admit that he was wrong? Luther refused.

After the meeting, Luther's friends heard rumors that Cajetan had ordered the monk's arrest. In the middle of the night, Luther fled to safety on horseback.

Shortly after Luther's return home, the aggressive efforts to get Luther to Rome stopped. The Pope's attention turned to another matter. On January 12, 1519, Emperor Maximilian of the Holy Roman Empire died. One of Europe's rulers must be elected as the next emperor. Only seven powerful men, called electors, had the right to vote. Luther's protector, Frederick the Wise, was one of the seven. Naturally, the Pope did not want to upset Frederick at this crucial time. He hoped to advise the prince's vote! As a result, Luther was not carried to Rome in chains and his writings continued to spread throughout Europe.

On June 28, 1519 when Charles V of Spain was elected emperor, Luther was still living and teaching in Wittenberg.

By this time, several other professors at the university had joined Luther in his attempt to reform the church. Wittenberg had become a center for Lutheran teaching. The school had become a popular university because students from all over Germany wanted to learn from Luther and his fellow professors.

In July of 1519, a professor from Ingolstadt named John Eck invited the Wittenberg professors to debate him in Leipzig. They accepted. Over two hundred men traveled to the debate. Many were students carrying weapons! These were turbulent years in Germany's history. Luther's travels held particular dangers because so many people opposed his vocal drive for reform. His perilous situation even led some German knights to offer their protection to Luther, but he never accepted.

No one doubted the danger of Luther's position. Everyone still remembered John Hus who had been burned at the stake one hundred years earlier. He was declared a heretic because he attacked some of the teachings of the Catholic Church.

Does this sound familiar? Professor Eck thought it did! During the debate at Leipzig, he stated that Luther taught the same heresy as Hus. Luther loudly denied the accusation! Like most Germans, he had been taught that Hus was a dangerous heretic.

During a break in the debate, Luther visited the library to read about Hus. What he discovered surprised him. Luther returned to the debate and shocked the audience by declaring that Hus had held many valid Christian beliefs.

Luther made another important statement at Leipzig. He claimed that he would believe a common man with a Bible before he would believe a Pope who ignored the Bible. Luther had begun to think that he must separate from the Pope. Eck attacked such ideas. "Are you the only one that knows anything?" he asked. "Except for you is all the Church in error?" [2] The debate continued for eighteen days and the two professors reached no agreement.

When Luther returned home, he continued the debate in writing. Throughout these years his understanding of Scripture continued to develop. Many of his reformation ideas were not formed until after the posting of his *Ninety-Five Theses*. As he learned, he taught others. He was a powerful writer and regularly sent manuscripts to the printer. His works were read with great interest in poor houses as well as castles. In Germany, a restless discontent with both the church and government had been brewing for years. Luther's writings voiced thoughts and struggles that a variety of people recognized as similar to those that stirred in their own hearts.

In 1520, church leaders in Rome prepared a bull of excommunication. A bull is an official proclamation from the Pope, and this particular one declared Luther an enemy of the church. It commanded bishops to seize and burn his books and demanded that Martin Luther admit his teachings were false. If

---

[2] Quoted in Roland H. Bainton, *Here I Stand: A Life of Martin Luther* (New York: Meridian, 1995), 91.

the monk did not admit his wrong within sixty days, he must be captured and delivered to Rome for punishment.

When the sixty days were up, Luther marched outside the Wittenberg gate with a group of professors and excited students. There, on the banks of the Elbe River, he burned the Pope's bull. By this action, Luther and his followers declared separation from the Catholic Church.

The increasingly tense situation in German society had captured the attention of the newly elected emperor, Charles V. The young ruler held firm Catholic beliefs, yet he did not immediately ship Luther to Rome as the papal bull commanded. He instead agreed to a request by Prince Frederick that Luther be examined in Worms, Germany at the upcoming Imperial Diet, the parliamentary body of the Holy Roman Empire. In the months preceding Luther's arrival, additional German leaders gave their support to this plan and recommended that the emperor promise to keep Luther safe.

Just getting to Worms required determination and courage. Luther traveled for two weeks. Many people warned him to turn around. Even though he had been promised safety, the emperor still might declare Luther a heretic and burn him at the stake. But Luther declared that his life was in God's hands, and he rode onward.

When he reached Worms on April 16, a group of excited knights rode out to meet the monk, and a crowd gathered at the gates to greet him. The emperor himself had not received such a welcome!

The next day, Luther appeared before the emperor. When asked to recant, his confidence wavered, and he asked for one more day to consider his answer. He wanted to be sure he said the right words. His request was granted.

On April 18, 1521, curious citizens again clogged the streets of Worms as the famous Wittenberg monk passed. Luther had to slip through houses and private gardens to safely reach his destination.

At last, he stood before Emperor Charles V and the Diet and spoke the words which would be remembered for centuries, "I cannot and I will not retract anything, since it is neither safe not right to go against conscience. I cannot do otherwise, here I stand. May God help me, Amen. "[3] Unless persuaded by the Bible itself that he was wrong, Martin Luther could not deny God's gift of salvation. He willingly faced probable death, confident that heaven awaited him.

Amazingly, Luther left Worms alive. He traveled wearily homeward, uncertain of whether death, banishment, or something else awaited him. Suddenly, a band of armed men galloped out of the woods. Many people had feared that Luther would be killed as he traveled home. Now, it seemed the dreaded moment had come. Swords flashed and strong men pulled Luther to the ground. Soon the attackers disappeared into the woods carrying Luther with them.

And so, Luther mysteriously vanished. People throughout Germany wondered whether he was alive or dead. Where could he be hidden? Almost no one knew.

---

[3] Quoted in Stephen J. Nichols, *Martin Luther: A Guided Tour of His Life and Thought*, 42.

The night following the attack, a tired group of travelers rode up a ridge to the massive Wartburg Castle. They left one lonely man behind. During the months that followed, the visitor wore the clothing of a knight and grew a long beard to cover his face. Unlike a typical knight, he spent most of his time writing. Can you guess his name? Martin Luther, of course! Frederick had arranged the secret capture of his famous professor so the reformer might safely hide in one of his secluded castles.

Luther certainly needed protection. Soon after he left Worms, the emperor signed the Edict of Worms. This imperial document was similar to the pope's bull. It declared Luther a heretic and placed him under the ban of the empire. The edict branded Luther an outlaw and commanded the destruction of his writings.

Luther spent nearly a year in hiding. In the lonely, drafty castle high above the town of Eisenach, he struggled with doubts, discouragement, and illness. He escaped idleness by writing. During this time, he labored on a project he hoped would open God's Word to the German people: he translated the entire New Testament into German. Later he would also translate the Old Testament. At last, any German who could read could also study the Bible!

During Luther's absence, his fellow reformers led the Lutheran Church that had recently separated from Rome. For years this group of men had criticized the Catholic Church; now they had the opportunity to design a church based on the Bible's teaching. Luther tried to give directions through letters to his Wittenberg friends. Everyone agreed that many changes were needed, and some men attempted to fix everything at once. Soon, life in Wittenberg became confusing and violent. Students smashed church statues and reformers made changes to the mass. Citizens who were used to the traditions of the Catholic Church were shocked.

Luther's worried friends wrote to him, and reportedly the town council sent him an invitation to come back to Wittenberg. Luther decided he must return to guide the fledgling church. He could hide no longer. If capture came, then he would accept his probable death.

In 1522, Luther returned to Wittenberg. Excitement filled the town. Luther worked immediately to calm the situation. His sermons warned that not everything should change at once. The leaders must be wise. They must prepare the people by preaching from the Bible.

Luther did agree that many changes were needed. For example, he encouraged priests and monks to marry! Many monks and nuns who supported reform desired to live beyond the walls of their monasteries. In 1523, Luther helped twelve nuns escape from a nearby convent. Since this was illegal, Luther's friend hid the women in a delivery wagon and drove them out of the gates to freedom. A few returned to their homes. The rest fled to Wittenberg where Luther attempted to find homes for them. Many of the younger ones married, and in the end only one remained – Katherine von Bora.

Martin Luther's friends saw an opportunity for him to follow his own advice. He should marry her himself! Luther disagreed. A man who might be burned at the stake would not be a good husband! In the end, he did marry Katherine on June 13, 1525. Although he told friends that he did not love her on their wedding day, the passing years softened his heart and his words. He later declared that he loved his Katie.

Luther's marriage took place during a turbulent year. The bloody Peasants' War of 1525 subjected Germany to a wave of uprisings which pitted commoners against landlord rulers in a horrifying slaughter. Men who felt oppressed by the nobles of Europe wished to fan the flames of religious change into a sweeping fire of reform that would change both society and politics as well. These men wanted freedom in society just as Luther had preached freedom from sin. Luther soon found his own reputation entangled in the angry emotions of the day. As the first uprisings began, Luther's writings were trumpeted by rebels who believed Luther supported their cause. Luther's responded with a harshly written rebuke. The sting of his sharp sentiments fueled debates about Luther's character which have continued to this day. When his words were first printed, Luther faced accusations from all sides. Princes blamed him for causing rebellion, commoners called him a traitor, and both enemies and friends questioned the wisdom of his published opinions on the conflict. Further attempts to defend his position actually caused criticism against him to increase.

Also in 1525, Luther penned a work of a different nature. *The Bondage of the Will* challenged the opinions of a famous professor named Erasmus. When completed, Luther considered this discussion of human freedom and God's sovereignty to be one of his most important writings. He asserted that God is the one who works salvation in the life of his people; no one can trust in self or good works to reach heaven.

*The Bondage of the Will* also gives another glimpse of the brash side of Luther which so infuriated his enemies. He outlined biblical proof for his position while accusing Erasmus of both "utter ignorance" and reading the Bible "sleepily."[4] Language such as this sometimes concerned even Luther's supporters.

In 1529, Luther devoted his attention to a book especially for children. He wanted to help parents teach their sons and daughters the basic beliefs of Christianity, so he wrote a series of questions and answers to clearly present the information. The resulting book, *The Small Catechism*, is still used today. Luther once said that he would not mind if the Pope burned all his books except for *The Small Catechism* and *The Bondage of the Will*.

Perhaps Luther worked on children's books because he had become a father himself! Martin and Katherine Luther had six children of their own and also raised four orphaned relatives. They lived in the old Black Cloister which Prince Frederick had given to them as a wedding gift. This building with its tall clock tower and many rooms had once been home to Wittenberg's monks, and Luther had lived there ever since his arrival in Wittenberg.

The large house stayed full. During the plague, the Luthers turned their house into a hospital and cared for many

[4] Martin Luther. "The Bondage of the Will." In *Martin Luther: Selections from His Writings*, ed. John Dillenberger (New York: Anchor Books, 1962), 174, 176.

suffering people. Luther believed that a pastor must be willing to risk death in order to care for the people in his town. In healthy years, travelers often spent the night, and many students boarded at the Black Cloister. The large building also had several lecture halls in which Luther taught.

Some of his most entertaining teaching, however, happened at his dinner table. On a typical night, friends and students gathered to eat and listen. Luther was usually talkative, and students began to write down his most interesting comments. After Luther died, these students published *Table Talk*. This collection of their notes provides a peek at the everyday Luther. Obviously, he loved to discuss theology, but he also commented on daily life. He was humorous, friendly and, at times, crude and critical.

Not only did Luther love to talk, he loved to sing. In his lifetime, he wrote nearly forty hymns. In many ways, Luther's most famous hymn, "A Mighty Fortress is Our God," illustrates his life. As a young man, this monk tried desperately to live a holy life. Finally, he admitted this task was impossible. *"Did we in our own strength confide, our striving would be losing...."* He could never be good enough! Instead, he must trust in the Savior whom God had provided. *"Dost ask who that may be? Christ Jesus, it is He...."* Even today, we can imagine Luther joyfully shouting out these words as he sang. He had struggled with fears and faced great danger. *"And though this world, with devils filled, should threaten to undo us, we will not fear, for God hath willed His truth to triumph through us...."* Luther risked his life to stand for truth. *"The body they may kill: God's truth abideth still, His kingdom is forever."*

Men did not kill Luther's body. Even though he lived as an outlaw during the years after the Diet of Worms, his enemies never captured him. Illness caused his death. In the winter of 1546, he traveled to Eisleben to help solve a disagreement. During this trip to his birthplace, he became terribly sick. He died a few days later on February 18, 1546. His body was returned to Wittenberg. There, this man who had done so much to start the Reformation was buried in the Castle Church where he had first taken his stand for the gospel.

*About the author:*

Kathleen L. Jacobs is a writer and homeschooling mother. She lives in Charlotte, North Carolina with her husband and four children. She particularly delights in sharing her love of history and writing with her family. While she worked on this biography of Martin Luther, the entire family learned about the Reformation and participated as manuscript critics! Her first historical novel, *Never Forsaken*, relates the challenges and joys experienced by a German family as they immigrate to America from a town near the birthplace of Martin Luther.

# Glossary of Words

**Abbot** – Leader of a monastery for men.

**Alcove** – A recess in the wall of a room.

**Annul** – To bring to nothing; to cancel or abolish.

**Antimony** – A toxic crystalline chemical element. The metallic form is silver-white, brittle, and lustrous; used in alloys.

**Apprentice** – Someone who works under a skilled professional in order to learn an art, craft, or trade.

**Archbishop** – A bishop of high rank.

**Auroch** – Large, long-horned European wild ox that became extinct in 1627.

**Autocracy** – A government based on one person having unlimited power.

**Bastides** – Well fortified strongholds for shelter during battle.

**Bier / Funeral Bier** – A wooden frame on which a corpse or a coffin is carried to where it will be buried.

**Bishop** – A Catholic clergy-man, ranked higher than a priest.

**Breeches** – Pants that end above the knee.

**Bubonic Plague** – An infectious and fatal epidemic disease caused by a bacteria transmitted by fleas and characterized by fever, chills, and the formation of swellings (buboes).

**Canonized** – Declared an official authorized saint.

**Carolingian Minuscule** – The writing style developed by Alcuin. This script was clear, concise, and uniformed. It consisted of both upper and lower case lettering and became the foundation for the present Roman alphabet. Named Carolingian because it was related to the Frankish dynasty, dating from 613 -987 AD.

Cauldrons – A large kettle, often made of iron; used over an open fire.

Chancellor – In Great Britain, a high official invested with judicial powers, in charge of all letters and writings of the monarch.

Chamlet – Cloth made of wool or silk and goat's hair.

Chaplain – A clergyman attached to a chapel, as of a royal court, prison, etc.

Chemise – A woman's one-piece undergarment, usually a straight dress.

Codpiece – A flap for the crotch of men's breeches.

Consanguinity – The relation or connection of people who descend from the same ancestor; blood relationship.

Consecration – To make or declare sacred.

Coronation – The crowning of a king.

Cuisse – A piece of armor covering the front of the thigh.

Dais – A raised platform in a large hall.

Dauphin – The eldest son of a King of France.

Degree – A title given by a university to a student who has completed a required course of study.

Dialectic – The process or art of reasoning by the discussion of conflicting ideas.

Dignitary – A person holding a high, dignified position or office in the Church or government.

Doublet – A man's close fitting jacket.

Dowager – A widow with a title or property derived from her late husband; a dowager queen is thus set apart from the new queen, the wife of her husband's successor.

Duchy – A dukedom, the territory or domains of a duke or duchess.

Dysentery – Any of various intestinal diseases characterized by inflammation, abdominal pain, toxemia, and diarrhea.

Entourage – A group of attendants or followers of an important person.

Epiphany – An appearance or manifestation of deity (God).

Feast of the Epiphany – January 6, also known as Twelfth Night and Kings' Day, a yearly Church festival celebrating the appearance of Jesus as Christ to the three kings, or wise men, in Bethlehem.

Fishmonger – Someone who sells fish to eat in the marketplace.

Garrison – A military post.

Gauntlets – Protective gloves that extend above the wrist.

Gothic – A style of architecture common in Western Europe beginning in the 12th century.

Grammar – The study of language, its proper use and style.

Greave – A piece of leg armor worn below the knee.

Heirloom – Something valuable that has been in the possession of a family for a long time and has been passed on from one generation to the next.

Heretic – A person who claims to follow a particular religion but holds beliefs that oppose the established truths of that religion.

Hurdy-gurdy – A square, wooden instrument in which the sound is made by turning a crank.

Illumination – A colored letter, design, or illustration decorating a manuscript or page; or the art or act of decorating written texts.

Incantations – Verbal charms or spells to produce magic.

Indulgences – A removal of punishment for sin that is granted by the Catholic Church, usually dependent upon a required act of faithfulness.

Infidel – A person who does not believe in a certain religion (to a Muslim, a Christian is an infidel; to a Christian, a Muslim is an infidel).

Liege lord – A feudal lord, a sovereign who rules over a vassal.

Lieutenant – A representative of another who performs a duty.

Lute – A stringed instrument.

Mausoleum – A tomb that is more ornate than the average, usually designed for a great or royal family.

Mead – A beverage made from fermented honey and water.

Merovingian Script – The writing style that consisted of untidy lettering that ran letters, words, and sentences together, making the reading of books difficult. Try this experiment. Take a half sheet of paper and write a letter to someone, using all capital letters, as well as not using any spaces between your words or sentences. How easy was it to read your letter? This difficulty was overcome with Alcuin's new script, Carolingian minuscule.

Minstrel – In the Middle Ages, a lyric poet and singer who traveled from place to place, singing or reciting, often with a harp or a lute.

Mint – A place where the coins used in a currency are manufactured under government supervision.

Monarchy – A country ruled by a monarch, usually a king or queen, who holds the position and power for life and by hereditary right.

Monastery – A house or community for people living together under religious vows.

Mosaic – A picture or design made with small pieces of colored material such as glass or tile stuck onto a surface.

Mutton – meat from a mature domestic sheep.

Nakers – Kettle drums.

Nuptials – A marriage ceremony.

Papal interdiction – An order from the Pope (the head of the Roman Catholic Church) banning a person or a group of people from the sacraments.

Parchment – The skin of an animal processed for the use of writing material.

Pauldron – A piece of armor covering the shoulder.

Pennon – A long, narrow ribbon-like flag.

Pilgrim – A person who travels to a shrine or holy place as an act of religious devotion.

Pilgrimage – The journey of the person travelling to a shrine or holy place.

Pontiff – Another name for the Pope, the religious head of the Catholic Church.

Pottage – A thick soup or stew of vegetables and sometimes meat.

Priestess – A woman who presides over religious rites in pagan religions.

Prophetess – In pagan religions, a woman who predicts the future.

Pumice – A light, porous volcanic rock, used for the process of smoothing and polishing.

Purgatory – A place where, according to Roman Catholic teaching, the souls of forgiven sinners will receive punishment for sins before entering heaven.

Quadrivium – The four liberal arts of study, consisting of arithmetic, music, geometry, and astronomy, originating in ancient Rome and continued through the Middle Ages.

Recant – To declare that one's past statements were wrong.

Refectory – The dining hall of a convent or monastery.

Regent – A person who carries out the duties of a king or other hereditary while that ruler is too young, out of the country, or physically or mentally unable to do so.

Relics – Items connected to the life of a saint or martyr.

Rhetor – The teacher of rhetoric.

Rhetoric – The study of writing or speaking as a means of communication or persuasion.

Sabaton – A piece of armor worn on the foot, made of chain mail with a solid toe and heel.

Senator – An elected or appointed member of the senate, which was the highest council of the ancient Roman Empire.

Seneschal – The steward or manager of the estate, especially in the medieval times.

Scepter – A staff carried by a king as an emblem of authority.

Shawm – A double-reed wind instrument like an oboe.

Shroud – A cloth in which a dead body is wrapped before burial.

Sisyphus – The legendary king of Corinth who was condemned to roll a bolder uphill each day, only for it to roll down each night, making his work endless.

Transepts – The projecting ends of a church that is shaped like a cross.

Treaty – An agreement made between two governments; the document signed for the agreement.

Threshing – Separating seeds or grain from the husks and straw by beating them with a flail. A flail has a long wooden handle and a shorter, free-swinging stick attached to its end.

Trivium – The three liberal arts of study, consisting of grammar, rhetoric, and logic, originating in ancient Rome and continued through the Middle Ages.

Troubadour – In the Middle Ages, a lyric poet or poet-musician who wrote poems and ballads of love and chivalry.

Tunic – A knee-length belted garment.

Vagrants – A person who does not have a job and wanders from place to place.

Vambrace – A piece of armor covering the forearm.

Vassal – In the Middle Ages, a person who held land under the feudal system, paying honor and loyalty and military service to an overlord in return for protection.

Vellum – High quality parchment made from calfskin, kidskin, or lambskin.

Vespers – The evening prayer service, often with an emphasis on thanksgiving.

# Timeline of Characters from

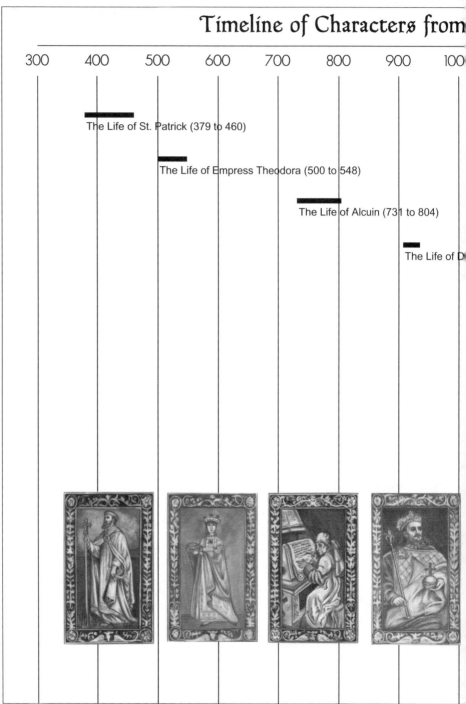

| 300 | 400 | 500 | 600 | 700 | 800 | 900 | 100 |
|-----|-----|-----|-----|-----|-----|-----|-----|

The Life of St. Patrick (379 to 460)

The Life of Empress Theodora (500 to 548)

The Life of Alcuin (731 to 804)

The Life of D

Timeline of Characters from the Middle Ages

* Timeline created using Easy Timeline Creator - for more information, visit
www.timelinecreator.com

# Middle Ages

| 1100 | 1200 | 1300 | 1400 | 1500 | 1600 |

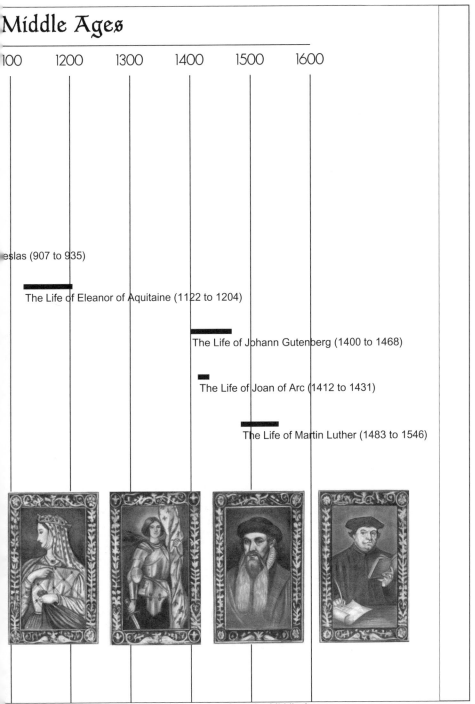

eslas (907 to 935)

The Life of Eleanor of Aquitaine (1122 to 1204)

The Life of Johann Gutenberg (1400 to 1468)

The Life of Joan of Arc (1412 to 1431)

The Life of Martin Luther (1483 to 1546)

Timeline of Characters from the Middle Ages

** Maps in this book were created by Knowledge Quest, Inc. - for more information, visit www.knowledgequestmaps.com

*About the Illustrator:*

 Darla Dixon is an illustrator based in the Atlanta area who specializes in portraiture. She maintains a busy schedule with a commissioned portrait and illustration service. Darla is married and the mother of three children, Alison, Sarah, and Keith. She is expecting baby number four any day now... Visit her website at www.darladixon.com.

# KNOWLEDGE QUEST ORDER FORM

**To order additional copies or find out more about our other great medieval products, log on to www.knowledgequestmaps.com and order some of the coordinating products below.**

Please fill out this form and mail it along with check, money order or cc information
to Knowledge Quest, Inc., P.O. Box 474, Boring, OR 97009-0474

Name

Address

City/State/Zip

Phone #                                                          Email

| Qty | Item # | Product Description | Price for each | Amount |
|-----|--------|---------------------|----------------|--------|
|     | 4002 | What Really Happened During the Middle Ages | $15.95 | |
|     | 1002+ | Blackline Maps of the Middle Ages | $14.90 | |
|     | 1010 | Blackline Maps of World History - The Complete Set (binder) | $39.95 | |
|     | 1011 | Blackline Maps of World History - The Complete Set (CD-ROM) | $29.95 | |
|     | 2002 | Story of the World, Vol 2 - The Middle Ages | $14.95 | |
|     | 2012 | Story of the World, Vol 2 - Activity Book | $24.95 | |
|     | 2020 | Story of the World, Vol 2 - Audiobook | $44.95 | |
|     | 3005 | Easy Timeline Creator (timeline creation software) | $29.95 | |
|     | 3008 | History Through the Ages timeline figures for Middle Ages | $19.95 | |
|     | 3010 | History Through the Ages - The Collection on CD-ROM | $74.95 | |
|     | 3030 | Wonders of Old: A Blank Timeline Book | $21.95 | |
|     | 3031 | Wonders of Old on CD-ROM | $21.95 | |
|     | 3021 | Wall Timeline of Medieval History | $17.95 | |
|     |      | Shipping for orders $10 - $30 is $2.75 | Subtotal | |
|     |      | Shipping for orders $30 - $100 is $4.75 | Shipping & Handling | |
|     |      | Shipping for orders over $100 is 6% of total | Total | |

Orders are shipped USPS Media mail. For an alternate shipping method (Priority
or UPS), email: orders@knowledgequestmaps.com to request S&H rates.
Or you may call us at (877)540-2030
*Checks should be made out to* **Knowledge Quest, Inc.**

Name on credit card (Visa/Mastercard/Discover/American Express)

Credit Card#                                                   Exp. Date